G000091078

How to be Perfect

How to be Perfect

A treasury of tips from a vicarage goddess

CATHERINE FOX

MONARCH
BOOKS

Mill Hill, London and Grand Rapids, Michigan

Copyright © Catherine Fox 2003.
The right of Catherine Fox to be identified as author of
this work has been asserted by her in accordance with the
Copyright, Designs and Patents Act 1988.

Published by Monarch Books in the UK 2003,
Concorde House, Grenville Place, Mill Hill, London NW7 3SA.

Illustrations by Bridget Gillespie

Distributed by:
UK: STL, PO Box 300, Kingstown Broadway,
Carlisle, Cumbria CA3 0QS;
USA: Kregel Publications, PO Box 2607,
Grand Rapids, Michigan 49501.

ISBN 1 85424 636 4 (UK)
ISBN 0 8254 6234 7 (USA)

All rights reserved.
No part of this publication may be reproduced or
transmitted in any form or by any means, electronic
or mechanical, including photocopy, recording or any
information storage and retrieval system, without
permission in writing from the publisher.

Unless otherwise stated, Scripture quotations are
taken from the Holy Bible, New International Version,
© 1973, 1978, 1984 by the International Bible Society.
Used by permission of Hodder and Stoughton Ltd.
All rights reserved.

British Library Cataloguing Data
A catalogue record for this book is available
from the British Library.

Designed and produced for the publisher by
Gazelle Creative Productions,
Concorde House, Grenville Place, Mill Hill,
London NW7 3SA.

Printed in Great Britain.

For my Kiwi friends,
especially Graham and Nancy,
in whose house most of this book was written.
With love and thanks.
Whakamoemititia a Ihowa.

CONTENTS

INTRODUCTION

There are so many How To books out there. How to Eat, How to Cook, How to Have Thin Thighs the Spiritual Way, How to Keep Smiling During Worship Songs You Hate – really, the list goes on for ever. So much instruction, so little time. I decided it would be a kindness to my fellow believers to write a straightforward, comprehensive guide to being perfect. All you need to know, handily contained in one set of covers, all at a very affordable price. Throw away all your other handbooks! Apart from your Bible, of course.

You will notice that I have subtitled this work "A Treasury of Tips". This is to reflect the paradoxical nature of life in the Vicarage – it is full of treasure, but it is generally a complete tip.

Enjoy! as they say these days. And just to be on the safe side, after you have enjoyed (if you come from a very strict Evangelical background), repent!

PART I

The perfect home

Introduction

In this section we look at what goes to make up the perfect home. I undertake this fully aware that I am lucky to have a home at all.

In the olden days the Book of Common Prayer had intercessions which could be said in the face of a variety of disasters: "Dearth and Famine", "War and Tumults", "Plague or Sickness". From many of these we are now fairly well shielded in the West. But mental health problems and slipping through the cracks in the pavement of the Welfare State – these are issues worthy of a prayer. Homelessness is not as distant as we like to think. And this thought is probably our best defence against the tyranny of home improvement.

This is not a guide to the perfect House Beautiful. It rests instead in the premise that the only way to get a perfect home is to be perfectly happy with the home you've got. I am perfectly capable of telling you how to go about this, not because I'm perfectly happy myself, but because, frankly, I'm a bit bossy.

CHAPTER 1
The perfect kitchen

Kitchens are a huge growth industry at the moment. Take a look in your nearest newsagents and you will see countless publications devoted to making you dissatisfied with the perfectly adequate kitchen you possess. What a lot of ordinary Christians don't realise is that there is a sinister agency behind this, controlling our perceptions of what constitutes a perfect kitchen. In their evil and quite possibly demonic way these people manipulate us into lusting after granite work surfaces, or Shaker units, or quarry tiles. They have us quivering for certain colour schemes and fabrics so that we cannot rest until we have ripped out the old despised oak effect cupboards, purged ourselves of dark green accessories and replaced them with blonde wood and softly gleaming chrome. You may think that this will make you feel better, that once the French cast iron saucepan-shaped hole in your life is filled you will be complete, but the truth is, you will never be satisfied. Within two years your dream kitchen will start to look dated and the whole ghastly cycle will start all over again.

I am able to see this with such dispassionate clarity because I know that I will never be in a position to commission a perfect kitchen of my own. One of the advantages of being married to a vicar and living in church accommodation is that you are free from the kind of relentless acquisitiveness which dogs the lives of ordinary homeowners. We are liberated from worry and able to operate on a purely spiritual plane, way above such petty considerations as kitchen floor coverings.[1]

---

1. As far as choice goes on the subject of kitchen flooring in the vicarage, you basically get one: that between liking and lumping. Very, very occasionally you happen to be the occupant when, for some unforeseen reason, the lino needs replacing (floor disappeared down mineshaft, or something). You will then be presented with a bewildering array of options between dirt brown and sludge green.

Furthermore, I find myself totally free from any unattractive envy when leafing through *House Poncified* magazines. I don't find myself in *any way* hoping the homeowners give themselves a hernia lifting their heavy French cast iron frying pan, just as it never so much as crosses my mind in an embittered way to wonder what my life might have been if I'd had the foresight to marry money, or make some of my own. And I thank God for that.

Platitude for the day

"The Art of Cooking is Cooking from the Heart." You could do worse than embroider that in cross-stitch, and hang it on your kitchen wall. Here, for instance, just off the top of my head, are three worse things you could do:

- maim an innocent defenceless creature
- trick old ladies out of their life savings
- advise small children to play on motorways

The list of *better* things you could do, is, of course, limitless; starting with kneeling on drawing pins and scouring your teeth with wire wool.

The purpose of the perfect kitchen

Let's get back to basics. What is a kitchen *for*? Well, there are as many answers to this as there are people. There is a certain section of society which believes that a kitchen is the place where you drop your muddy football kit and leave it so it can miraculously revert to its clean and ironed state. A literalist might reply "a kitchen is for cooking in"; while a sentimentalist might counter "a kitchen is the warm beating heart of the building, which turns a house into a home". Whereupon the literalist might justifiably smack the sentimentalist round the head with the *Concise Oxford Dictionary*, before pointing to the entry for kitchen, which reads "Part of house where food is cooked". I'll tell you an interesting fact about the *Concise Oxford Dictionary*, by the way. It does not have the word "gullible" in it. When someone told me that, I didn't believe them, so I looked it up.

So at rock bottom, whatever else you may do in your kitchen, if you never cook in it, it is not truly a kitchen.

The perfect cooker

The first thing to grasp about cookers (you may prefer to call them "stoves" or "ovens") is that they are all individuals and equipped with distinct personalities. It's always as well to bear this in mind before you approach one and attempt to cook something on it. Like any relationship, if you start off on the wrong foot it may take a while before any misunderstandings are sorted out and the partnership can progress in any meaningful way. I say this as one who has never had to buy my own cooker. Alas, all the cookers I have ever had to deal with have been other people's exes. With all that history and hurt, it's not surprising that things frequently get off to a bumpy start.

In particular, I remember one slim-line, rather suave looking ceramic hobbed electric oven that had belonged to my Grandma. To be honest, I found it very temperamental and prima donna-ish, and we never did get along, really. I suppose this was the legacy of it never having truly been appreciated by my Gran. It had been foisted on her by my parents who split her up from her beloved gas cooker, after it became clear she could no longer be trusted to handle the relationship responsibly. (By then she had no sense of smell and a certain vagueness when it came to turning things off.)

Thought for the day

My friends, there is no such thing as a perfect cooker. It's no use waiting for the Mr Right of the hob world to appear and sort out all your problems. No matter how flash your stove may look in the showroom, you will still have to work at your cooking.

The perfect fridge

The perfect fridge *du jour* is the pastel-coloured ironic retro 50s-look fridge. If you are lucky enough to possess one, well, more fool you. It will date in a couple of years and people will secretly sneer at you for being a hopeless domestic appliance fashion victim. I say this out of compassion, not envy. Next time buy an ordinary cheap white one like everybody else.

I adopt this brisk tone because it is all too easy to become fixated on fridges and freezers. It is worth taking time to stop and reflect that

"Well, the Chinese have managed without 'em on their sampans for millennia so how come I need a 6-ring non-stick stainless steel job with integral auto wok burner here?"

in Jesus' day there was no refrigeration. Indeed, the Bible has nothing to say on the subject, but as with many aspects of modern life, it is possible – nay, it is our duty – to seek out underlying biblical principles and eternal truths and see how they relate to the 21st century.

The eschatological implications of the refrigerator

Of all our domestic appliances it is the fridge that brings us closest to a day-by-day understanding of the End Things. When we contemplate the Last Judgement, we think, perhaps, of all the secrets of the heart being laid bare, of having to give an account of our lives. Our Puritan forebears took very seriously the possibility that each day might be their last. But in our modern hygienic relatively safe world, we often lose sight of our own mortality. This is where the humble fridge can help.

Contemplate, if you will, your own refrigerator. What does it contain? How happy would you be if some complete stranger were to march into your kitchen, wrench your fridge open and examine the contents with a pitiless eye? What would they find? Out-of-date yoghurts and mugs of chicken fat covered in cling film dating back to the late Middle Ages? One fossilised spoonful of apple crumble in an old margarine tub that you thought at the time (nine months ago) it would be a shame to throw away? A slime-filled package which once held baby spinach?

If this is the case, then don't despair. Treat your fridge as a parable. Personally, I find the idea of a clean fridge more helpful than the advice about wearing clean underwear in case you are run over. Think about it – for every time you are run over, how many people look in your fridge? You could go *years* without being run over, but there is a very real daily threat that a visitor, reaching for the milk, might discover the state of your vegetable rack. Yes, my friends, a dirty fridge is a constant reminder of the frailty of the human condition, and as such, it is to be cherished.

You may, of course, like to clean your fridge out now and then. This might help your general sense of well-being, for all I know. If it's raining, the car has broken down, the bills have all arrived together, you are feeling fat and useless, you will be able to tell yourself "At least my fridge is clean." Another strategy is to clean out *someone else's* fridge. This is always much more interesting than cleaning your own. For maximum satisfaction, do it without asking permission, as a prophetic enactment of free grace. It will *really* annoy them.

How to decorate your fridge properly

Provided you remember the important Christian maxim that the *outside* of your fridge doesn't matter, it's what's on the *inside* that counts, you are free to decorate your fridge as you choose. The overall effect should not appear contrived. It should be eclectic and look as though it has evolved casually over the weeks and months (even if you've worked quite hard to achieve this appearance of spontaneity).

As we go to press, my fridge is decorated with the following:

- 1 poster of John Calvin bearing the slogan "Total Depravity"
- 1 poster of George Clooney bearing the invisible slogan "Phworr!"
- A range of fridge magnets, including,
    Michaelangelo's David, complete with removable socks, boxer shorts and vest
    1 planet
    1 blue and yellow fish
    1 bear (which slides down the fridge)
    1 silver roller-blade boot
    5 wine bottles, one covering David's private parts
    2 mottos about friendship and/or chocolate
    Crosslinks – "God's Word for God's World" (for reasons of profanity, *not* to be used to cover David's private parts)
    1 Icon of Our Lady of Kykkos (ditto)
    1 Bruges town house
    1 letter P (or b) left over from alphabet set
    1 cross-stitched cup and saucer containing teabag and poem "I wish we could sit down together/and drink a cup of tea/But since we can't, when you have this one/I hope you'll think of me", kindly given me by a visiting pastor's wife from America

"There's nothing a bit off _in_ this fridge
so can we keep the _outside_ the same, please!"

> 1 cross-stitched gin bottle with poem, "I wish we could sit down together and have a slug of gin/But I'm of Nonconformist stock and think that booze is sin" (existing only in my imagination)
>
> 1 set of magnetic fridge poetry, currently arranged to read "My caterwaul was munificent/With so torpid a festoon"

- 6 postcards, including:

> 1 picture of courgettes (stuck on with David's boxer shorts)
>
> 1 view of Paris (from gloating fellow novelist writing book on rugby which appears to necessitate an inordinate amount of foreign travel and lunching)

- 4 photos, including:

> 1 of older son wearing High Court judge's robes and wig
>
> 1 of the curate, wearing white plastic thigh boots and union jack mini dress (from the joint Anglican/Roman Catholic March of Witness on last year's Cross-dressing Sunday)[2]

- 1 letter from the GP recommending my asthmatic son gets a flu jab, reassuringly informing him that EACH YEAR PEOPLE UNFORTUNATELY DIE FROM INFLUENZA.

Handy hint

Another good idea from a Pensions Advisor I know (other than "Get a pension, dumb dumb" – advice I have yet to follow) is to attach a whiteboard marker to your fridge so that you can scribble down your shopping list as you run out of things. This will also provide small children with a harmless opportunity to doodle. I don't do this myself, as I know that my children would harmlessly doodle bottoms on my fridge. A word of warning, though. Make sure you haven't bought an *indelible* marker by accident, or your fridge will forever say "Tampons" or "Decaffeinated Earl Grey teabags", or some other equally embarrassing thing.

---

2. Oh, all right then. That was just a spot of Nonconformist baiting. There's no such thing. Any cross-dressing urges find full expression through the normal outlets provided by vestments.

The well-appointed refrigerator

If you were to come and look in my fridge, I am proud to say that you would be instantly intimidated. It is quite scarily well ordered. I have achieved this by the simple expedient of buying a big fridge. The older, smaller fridge, used to provoke me into swearing horribly and violently (or *would* have done, if I knew any swear words, of course) each Friday as I tried to fit in the week's shopping. I ended up grovelling around for ages on my knees on the floor – what kind of position is *that* for the Christian woman? Well, apart from a *prayerful* one, I mean – as I attempted to fit in all the milk and cheese and veg. I used occasionally to burst into tears and shout "I hate this ******* fridge!"[3] In the end, worn down by the sight of so much misery, a VIK[4] agreed that we needed a new fridge. And freezer. Sorry? Didn't I mention we needed a new freezer as well, darling? I thought you realised!

We kept the old fridge and put it in the tool cupboard, drilling a hole through the wall so that we can plug it in in the kitchen. Well, drilling several holes, if we are being honest. It took a couple of attempts to meet up with the holes drilled from the other side. But hey, we are a vicar and a novelist, not a couple of civil engineers. We're not talking the channel tunnel here. No lives were lost. The old fridge has been re-designated "the champagne fridge". A VIK thinks it's the Beer fridge, but he's wrong about that.

Short-cuts to the perfect fridge

First, buy some fridge trays. You can get them from that catalogue that comes through your door and appears to be full of things you'd never want (telescopic long-handled mops for washing upstairs windows, oven shelf cleaner). These trays mean that you can put all the irritating little things (Babybels, fromage frais) all together in one place so they don't fall down the back and get lost for three generations.

Second, why not invest in a set of realistic-looking plastic

---

3. ******* stands for "stupid", in case you have always wondered what those rows of stars mean in newspapers. It can also denote "bother!" on occasion; and no, I don't know what the leftover asterisk is there for, either.

4. Vicar I Know.

vegetables? They will not grow mouldy, and your children are no less likely to eat them than they are the real thing.

Third, always leave room for gin. Make this a priority. Vodka can be kept in the freezer, of course, as it remains liquid at a lower temperature. You can't do this with gin. Well, you can, but you end up with a vast solid gin ice lolly. What's wrong with that? you might think. I'll tell you – you can't get it out of the bottle. This can be very frustrating.

CHAPTER 2
The perfect sitting room

A lounge by any other name

In England, what you call your sitting room will reveal a hideous amount about you and your ethnic origins and social aspirations.

I say sitting room, you say front room – let's call the whole thing off. My Grandma, like most good working-class people, used to have a Front Room. I suppose this is a helpful name in several ways. It tells you that the room is *situated towards the front of the house*, to lapse briefly into the language of rail announcements. It also tells you that it is *not for sitting in*. It's for laying out corpses and entertaining the clergy. In my Grandma and Grandad's case, it was also where the Christmas tree went, and for that reason I always called it "the Christmas room". The front room, or parlour, as I believe is the American equivalent, always contained the best furniture and was therefore too grand for every day use.

So there, at one end of the social spectrum, we have the Front Room. Coming in next, we have The Lounge, with its pretensions of upward mobility. And if you have a *lounge*, you will probably have a *settee*. If, on the other hand (creeping yet further across the spectrum) you have a *Sitting Room*, it will contain a *sofa*. If you are dead posh you will have a Drawing Room, not for drawing in, of course, but to which one may *withdraw* after dinner while the gentlemen drink port, smoke cigars and tell risqué stories.

Another interesting thing to note is that the posher you are, the more permissible it is to keep your lounge/sitting/drawing room in complete chaos. A Front Room has to be kept like a museum. It may even have protective plastic covers on the three piece suite. In a drawing room you might have to kick aside muddy riding boots, a fortnight's worth of the *Daily Telegraph* and a dozen corgis before sitting down on the tatty chintz-covered sofa.

And what about the term "Living Room"? Where does *that* fit in? I suggest it finds its place between Lounge and Sitting Room; but the whole thing, like the English Class system in general, is so sensitive and complex, that I hesitate to pronounce. There are pros and cons about the term living room. It usefully reminds us that the room is for *real* people living *real* lives – and, in many cases, making a real mess; but on the other hand it seems to suggest that there is a danger of falling lifeless to the floor in other areas of the house.

The perfect three-piece suite

I have a profound and unshakable belief that the perfect three-piece suite is white or cream. I am also unwavering in my opinion that to buy a white three-piece suite is folly if there are such things as Belgian chocolate, good coffee or red wine in your life. Not to mention small boys. I believe the technical term for this state of mind is "cognitive dissonance".

Maybe in heaven this tension will be resolved. Perfection on this poor fallen earth probably resides in taking the generous approach in life. In this case I suppose that would mean consulting other people's comfort as well as your own. There's not much point having a sitting room so perfect people are afraid to enter without removing their shoes and outer garments. Although for nudists, this would presumably constitute perfection. **But remember**: If the Good Lord had intended us to be nudists, he would not have given us wicker furniture.

Thought for the day

However much I hanker after a white sofa, I can't spend my life permanently poised with a can of stain remover and damp cloth waiting for a drip of coffee. Or swooping with coasters to protect my polished wood. It would be too exhausting. If you stop to think about it, God isn't too precious about the perfect world he made. He gives us space to tear about and mess it up, chop the trees down, kill the whales and so on. His sun still rises and sets on the just and the unjust alike. This doesn't mean he's without sorrow and without plans, and is not at all times and in all places patiently working and scheming and renewing in endlessly ingenious ways.

The sensible route with pale colours

I indulge my passion for cream in the realm of curtains (discounting cakes/puddings). But a tiny word of warning here: it costs more to have cream curtains dry-cleaned than it does to buy them in the first place. I discovered this when I took my sitting room curtains to our local cleaners. I blenched, I must confess, when I was told what it was going to cost, but wrote the cheque out bravely. What else could I do? Say "Actually, now I come to look, they aren't *that* dirty", and take them home again? "They must have been quite fashionable a few years ago, them cream curtains," observed the woman in the shop blightingly. "We used to get quite a few in."

Stripping

There are few utterances more quietly satisfying than "I'm just going to hire a stripper for the vicar." Actually, I don't hire a stripper, I borrow one from a midwife I know, who has all manner of scary power tools at her disposal. This is in her private, rather than her professional capacity; although, come to think of it, I have seen her dissect a cheesecake with a scalpel while wearing surgical gloves, so there is clearly some cross-over of skills going on in her life. I only borrowed her stripper to strip some window sills so craterous that even I couldn't blithely slap a coat of gloss over them. I did *not* use it to strip doors and skirting boards to reveal the original pine. That would be foolishness. In a few years time the big Wheel of Taste turns and stripped pine becomes unfashionable. You are then faced with the choice of repainting it (and you won't be able to bear the thought) or of being unfashionable. Think about it: stripped wood will go in and out of fashion with the years. There will always be times when you are out of date. Better to be out of date without the trouble of stripping the wood. Paint – you know it makes sense.

*"I don't care if it **DOES** do what it says on the tin, kindly give Mrs Philips the nappy for her baby."*

CHAPTER 3
The perfect bathroom

What is a bathroom?

This may strike you as a pointless question, but the matter is not as clear cut as many of us imagine. For example, if an American asks you where your bathroom is, you could (with faux innocence) direct them to a room containing a bath and a washbasin, and then amuse yourself for several minutes while your American guest struggles to re-phrase the question without actually using the word "lavatory".

In England a bathroom may or may not contain a loo. In the States it might not contain a bath. To be fair, the same is also true in the UK in these days of showering. En suite bathrooms, in particular, seldom have baths. "En suite upright coffin" would be a better description of some I have encountered. You have to plan ahead strategically and make sure you enter the right way. Turning round once you're in is not always an option. In fact, if you are heavily pregnant, my advice is don't go in at all.

Bathroom checklist

Your perfect bathroom should include at least six of the following:

- bath
- shower
- basin
- loo
- loo roll
- bidet
- sponge alphabet to stick on bath*

- towels on rails
- towels on floor*
- soap
- dish containing small soaps/sachets of shampoo pilfered from hotels
- dirty clothes in basket
- dirty clothes on floor*
- potty*
- headless Action Man*
- tub of nappy cream containing Action Man's head*
- wooden spoon
- snorkel*
- foetid flannels on corner of bath
- mirror
- amusing paperbacks
- cleaning equipment
- small wall cupboard full of embarrassing paraphernalia

* applies if you have children

You may be puzzling over why I have listed "wooden spoon". I've puzzled over that myself. We had one in our bathroom for several years. Once a visitor asked me about it, then instantly blushed to the roots of her hair. I have no idea what explanation suddenly presented itself to her, and I should love to know, because it sounds like fun. The real answer is probably boringly predictable, like the answer to the question "Why is there a king size duvet stuck in your cat flap?" Durr – because I have small children, of course.

Other people's bathrooms

There are certain bits of accepted *etiquette* surrounding the use of other people's bathrooms.

1. Snooping. It is terribly bad form to peer in the small cupboard to see what embarrassing items they contain, although everyone does it.

2. Fiddling. You should not rearrange the sponge letters in the bath so that they spell "bum",[1] or worse. (If, heaven forefend, there *are* any words worse than that! Don't ask *me*, I wouldn't know. I'm a vicar's wife).

3. Pilfering. Do not pilfer from the little dish containing fancy soaps/shampoos from hotels. Pilfering from hotels is fine. After all, you're paying the bill, aren't you? Pilfering pilfered items from friends is *not* fine. The soaps must remain unused and gathering dust in the dish until the Second Coming. You may try on the plastic shower cap if you like, but remember to take it off your head and replace it in the little dish before going back to join the other guests, or they may look at you a little strangely.

4. Sampling. ON NO ACCOUNT are you to try out any expensive cosmetics, shampoos, deodorants, sprays etc. This is most important. You cannot be certain what those swanky-looking bottles actually contain. For all you know your hostess may keep her moustache bleach in the little container marked "hand cream". And there's a risk you might dye your hair purple with that innocuous-looking gel, which would be a dead giveaway to your hosts that you've been nosily rummaging.

5. Drawing attention to low standards. Resist the temptation to rearrange your hosts' knick-knacks into a more pleasing order. This is very irritating, Mother. Similarly, don't write your name in the dust on the window sill. You may, if you wish, re-hang the loo roll if it is on the wrong way round. The proper way is with the roll-end hanging politely down at the front, not the back. It has been scientifically proved. Don't bother folding the first sheet into a point, unless you work in a hotel and can't help yourself. NEVER leave one sheet balanced on the empty cardboard tube so that the next person has to change the roll, either in your own home or in someone else's. This is despicable behaviour and those who practise it will never prosper.

---

1. When I was growing up we were never allowed to say "bum". In fact, my youngest sister heard the word so seldom she actually thought the obscenity in question was "pum". I can remember her staring at me in round-eyed shock once when I asked her to pass me the pumice stone.

Thought for the day

Are you wondering how to achieve bathroom perfection? My friends, you will never do this. There will always be a gulf between your personal vision of what your bathroom should be and what it actually is. This gulf is bridged by grace and forgiveness alone. Perfect bathrooms only exist in hotels, and even then just for one brief moment before some guest steps inside and starts using it, tearing off the neatly pointed loo roll end, wrecking the display of advanced level fancy towel-folding and stuffing the little soaps and sachets greedily into their sponge bag.

You may be thinking that *other people's* bathrooms often seem near-perfect. This is because they were down on their hands and knees half an hour before you arrived cleaning the floor behind the sink pedestal, scrubbing the porcelain and spraying various cleaning products into the air so that it all smells clean. Call in unannounced and you will be stepping over yesterday's underpants to reach the basin.

In an ideal world – perhaps in heaven, for all I know – everyone would have their own private bathroom and never have to share. To know that the only underpants you are stepping over are your own – if that is not perfection, I don't know what is.

My three top tips for improving an inadequate bathroom

- hire a professional cleaning firm
- open a bottle of champagne[2]
- wear a blindfold

What does the Bible teach about bathrooms?

The only mention of bathrooms I can call to mind is the Living Bible's now notorious translation "Saul went into the cave to go to the bathroom". Considering the King James version informs us that Saul went into the cave "to cover his feet", British mirth at our American friends' expense is a little unfair.

---

2. Improves most things.

CHAPTER 4
Bedrooms

The perfect bedroom contains a bed for sleeping in and the right number of people. I deliberately state this vaguely, because there is no "right" number of people to suit every set of circumstances. There are times when one would be lonely, others where two is too many. Still others, when two is well on the way to being perfect, and a small person who has just had a bad dream, makes a most unwelcome third. (Let the reader understand.)

Peace, perfect peace

Many of you will recognise this as the first line of a hymn. When my children were tiny, I was always struck by the wisdom of the line "Peace, perfect peace, *with loved ones far away*". To this day I assert a mother's right not to be climbed on whenever she sits down.[1]

Nowhere is peace more essential than in a bedroom. You don't have to have total silence – people are capable of getting used to express trains and low-flying aircraft – but it does have to be quiet enough for you to sleep. A bedroom you can't get to sleep in is no bedroom at all – genuine Victorian brass bedsteads and drifting muslin notwithstanding. In my experience it is sudden or erratic noises that do the damage; or noises which cause you to fear. When I was little I was scared of the ghost knocking in the cupboard. I was scared of it even after my Dad explained it was just the slates on the roof contracting after a hot day, and slipping slightly. In later years it was the sound of drunken voices and breaking glass that made me afraid. The other day my older son asked me what was the thing I most wanted from a house – perhaps with a view to becoming a famous

---

1. This is what play pens are for, incidentally. They are not for keeping children *in* – they howl if you try – but for keeping them *out*, while mother sits inside with a drink and a magazine for five minutes.

footballer and buying me one – and I replied, To feel safe in it. I have lived in vicarages where that was not the case. These days, fortunately, if there are naughty children marauding round the house in the dark, the chances are they are my own.

Helpful hint

Sometimes, if you catch it in time, you can choose not to let a particular noise get to you. You tell yourself you are not responsible for it, and that you will not let it disturb you. Failing that, try earmuffs. There are some people driven to distraction by the sound of church bells ringing. To them I would say, Move house. Durr! Didn't you notice the steeple looming over the garden wall when you bought the place? Personally, I love to hear church bells. It's part of our heritage. Even when they are so badly rung they sound like an ice cream van falling down a spiral staircase.

How to decorate the perfect bedroom

Decorate it *exactly how you like.* You are the one who will be spending time there. If you want a dark blue ceiling with luminous glow stars, go for it. Don't worry about what visitors will think. What business is it of theirs? If you feel happy with your bedroom a lot of other things will fall into place. Problems do sometimes arise when there is more than one person using the bedroom. I once undertook the job of creating an elaborate jungle in my sons' room. I was about halfway through when my younger son suddenly announced he didn't want a jungle at all, he wanted Outer Space. OK, I said, let's do half and half. No, said my older son, That would look stupid. Eventually we reached a sort of compromise where the room was a jungle and the inside of the bottom bunk was Outer Space. These days they have separate rooms, thank goodness, and both jungle and outer space alike are covered with a demure pale blue. I know this is a bit of a shame, but I didn't want guests to be scared by the painted snakes slithering out from behind the radiator. They might burst into my room saying they've had a bad dream.

The trickiest negotiations are, as ever, between partners. My impression is that most men will acquiesce to just about any interior design scheme for the sake of a quiet life and a spot of sex, provided it's not too frilly.[2] In some cases you can get away with a frilly bedroom, provided it's not pink as well. I bet you could get away with frilly *and* pink, plus little bowls of pot-pourri, and a row of cute teddy bears, provided you also got Sky TV and let him watch football in bed. Love, honour and negotiate is the motto here.

And now we draw perilously near to the Big Question:

How to have perfect sex

This is simple: be perfect yourself, select a perfect partner and go to it! Otherwise, you can't. Even in heaven you can't, if we are to be like the angels, neither marrying nor giving in marriage. And I don't *think* the Gospel writers wish us to conclude that extra-marital sex is therefore a goer in the afterlife.

As an earnest young woman I read various guides to Christian Married Love. I can remember one book describing a particular sexual position, then noting "This is seldom used." I pondered that. Seldom used by us, the authors, did it mean? Seldom used by Christians? *Only* used by depraved perverts? If so, why is it being described in these clean-living pages, and when can I have a go?

One of my favourite positions

First of all, relax. One person (it doesn't matter which, this can work with either partner on top) lies on their back with their legs apart. The other person is in a kneeling position between their partner's spread legs, and he or she reaches forward with either arm, towards the partner's neck. The prone partner takes a firm grip of the extended arm, pivots swiftly round to an angle of about 45 degrees (experiment to see what is most comfortable for you), then, still maintaining their hold on the arm, swings a leg clean over the person on top's head, which will then be gripped between the knees. Lean back, controlling the arm, which – unless the partner submits – will then break. This is called *ju-ji-gatame*. We do it in judo all the time. Don't try it at home unless you have an accredited coach present in your bedroom at all times.

---

2. The scheme, not the sex. By all means wear frills. Frills can work.

How to make a bed perfectly

Follow the instructions on the piece of paper from IKEA.

How to tell if a bed is properly aired

Put an upside down whisky tumbler between the sheets. Leave it for a few minutes. If, when you take it out, it looks a bit cloudy and blurred, then either the bed is not properly aired, or else you have drunk too much whisky.

CHAPTER 5
The cupboard under the stairs

I f we are embracing a literal fundamentalist approach, then the first step towards achieving the perfect cupboard under the stairs is to make sure you are not living in a bungalow or a flat. I personally believe that it is perfectly acceptable to be more liberal in your interpretation of the concept of "cupboard under the stairs". It need not actually be *under the stairs* in any concrete sense. What's important here is that we have grasped the timeless truth conveyed by the phrase "cupboard under the stairs", and allow it to shape our lives. In my opinion this is an area on which Christians may legitimately disagree. I hope I always try to be broadminded. I mean, some of my closest friends are narrow-minded fundamentalists.

How to achieve a perfect glory hole

A glory hole (or "tip" as we call it in the vicarage) may be located in any room, nook or cranny of the house where things may be deposited in a haphazard fashion, a door closed on it, and the whole mess forgotten. (See, for example, Chapter 6 The Perfect Attic/Loft, below.) In some cases an old curtain tossed over a heap of cardboard boxes may constitute a glory hole. Just because you are in cramped living quarters doesn't mean you cannot effectively operate a tip, or system of tips. Drawers may be mini glory holes, as indeed may the space under beds, on top of wardrobes or down the back of the sofa cushions. If you have small children, or better still, teenagers, let them guide you. This is one area (like understanding DVD players) where youngsters have a natural advantage.

Your glory hole checklist

A good glory hole should include

- broken items
- incomplete sets
- obsolete computers/electrical equipment
- polystyrene packaging
- carpet/lino offcuts
- hideous lamps/curtains
- bin liners full of grey babygrows/maternity clothes
- Christian paperbacks
- fondue set
- failed handicraft/DIY attempts

Getting the best out of your clutter

To achieve the best result, the occasional effort should be made at imposing order. The sense of chaos will be heightened if the person opening the cupboard can faintly discern the crushed remains of IKEA storage boxes, or clapped-out plastic crates.

How to stow clutter

A good rule of thumb when stowing items is to open the door, toss the broken kettle, or whatever, as far to the back of the pile as you can manage, then shut the door swiftly before the whole lot falls out on top of you (the Open, Toss, Slam system).

Thought for the day

Is there a part of your life which is a spiritual glory hole? Have you allowed a huge clutter of failures and unkept promises and broken deadlines to accumulate in your conscience? Are you haunted by that menacing phrase so often quoted in sermons, which advises you to Keep Short Accounts With God? You know you are. This is because you are an Evangelical. Whenever I hear people going on about the legacy of guilt a good Roman Catholic upbringing leaves you with, I ask myself, Have they ever tried being brought up an Evangelical? God the Keeper of Accounts – what kind of picture does that conjure up? Can we see him hunched over his ledger scribbling away "Aha! A lustful thought! And a little surge of covetousness. I saw them both and you can be sure I'm noting them down, sonny Jim!"?

"Don't blame me — they're the same disgusting colour as those cushions from Aunt Pru's drawing room."

But supposing that repository of failures which is the human conscience, isn't viewed like that by God? What if it's a treasure trove, the odds and ends of things which go to make up you in all your hopelessness and glory? I merely float this idea. Maybe it's a bit like coming across a cardboard box of things in the attic from your childhood. Old school books and diaries and letters from friends and posters of David Cassidy and so on?

My younger sister once came upon a five-year diary from when she was about eight. One page bore a single entry in block capitals: "CATHY IS A FAT, FAT PIG AND I HATE HER!" Neither of us can remember what provoked that outburst, although we are both pretty sure it was deserved. At this distance, though, neither of us is concerned by the rights and wrongs of the matter. It nicely encapsulates an era of intense sibling rivalry we've grown out of.[1] Now we laugh about it with forgiveness and indulgence. I suppose what I'm trying to say is that maybe this is a better model for God than that of the crabby I SAW THAT! note-taker.

Maybe there's nothing so broken and useless about us that it can't be taken up and treasured, or even put to some ingenious use. I have a friend who is a jeweller and she has what she calls her "Bit Box" where she chucks the experiments that go wrong. Every so often she has a rummage in it and picks out some failure or other and suddenly, years later, sees it in a new light and it becomes the starting point for some new and wondrous piece of jewellery.

Things you should not put in the cupboard under the stairs

Number one is *small children*. Small children really don't like being locked up in confined spaces, so please don't try it. This is because crocodiles, ghosts, the Childcatcher from Chitty Chitty Bang Bang and Lord Voldemort all lurk in dark places like cupboards, or gaps under beds, and this can be frightening. When I was small my sisters and I were terrified of Fierce Pappoons, and I'd have to say our fear was in no way alleviated by our father drawing a picture in chalk of a Fierce Pappoon in a dark corner of the shed where we liked to play.

---

1. Well, I have. She may not have done. But then, I always was more mature than her.

And just because the picture was of a spotted six-legged cow thing doesn't mean that it wasn't scary, because it was.

If children *voluntarily* go into the cupboard under the stairs, that's a different matter. A vicar's wife I know used to tell her small son not to pick his nose or fiddle with his person in public, because *people didn't like to watch little boys doing that* (she gave this reason so as not to instil a sense of guilt about normal bodily matters). He solved this by disappearing into the cupboard under the stairs whenever the need arose. She later told him not to say horrible things about his new baby sister, because mummy didn't like to hear her little boy saying that kind of thing. The following day she was walking down the hall and heard a small voice from the cupboard intoning "Kill Bethany! Kill Bethany!"

There are times when I need a cupboard for this kind of purpose. Actually, a padded cell would be even better. I could go in, rant, scream, fling myself about, then emerge five minutes later composed. Or "composted", as a VIK once accidentally typed in a pew sheet.

Other things not to put in the cupboard under the stairs

- school PE kit
- flammable material
- inflammable material[2]
- claustrophobics

---

2. Why aren't they opposites, I want to know?

CHAPTER 6
The perfect attic and cellar

Attics and lofts

The main difference between an attic and a loft is that an attic has proper stairs going up to it and proper floorboards when you get there. Try this simple test: if you gain access to the space in question by climbing precariously up a ladder and squeezing through a small hole not designed for the human frame to squeeze through, and then, when you finally get up, you promptly plunge through the floor up to your thigh in a gap between the rafters – if all this applies, then what you've got there is probably a loft.

An attic *could theoretically* be used as a proper room, whereas a loft is essentially a "tip" or "glory hole" (see Chapter 5 above), where you stow your artificial Christmas tree and decorations, your camping gear and anything that "may come in useful one day", but never does. Many people rather boringly use their attics as lofts. This is a shame. Attics are much better utilised as garrets for artists and writers to starve in; or if not precisely *starve*, at least resolve to cut down on chocolate digestive biscuits in. This certainly is how I use my attic.

The perfect attic

Allow me, if you will, to hold up my own attic as a perfect example of the genre. I had it specially transformed from loft to attic status by a boat builder I know. After making it clear to him that I didn't require portholes, gunwales, mains'ls, bilges, rowlocks, futtocks or any other maritime trappings useful on the high seas, but superfluous, on the whole, in a quiet suburban street in the West Midlands, he did a jolly good job.

A perfect attic needs to have wildly sloping ceilings so you can

43

pretend you are in the middle of Paris in the 19th century, and a little window to gaze out of pensively. My little window looks out across our street, affording me an excellent view of the speed camera and any motorists it catches speeding, and serve them right. I watch the trees and the birds, occasionally sighting a jay or a greater spotted woodpecker.[1] I can also see the man from down the road walking his scary Alsatian, the post woman coming up the drive, the Parcel Force van approaching, slowing, coming thrillingly to a halt in front of the house! then reversing and delivering a parcel to our neighbours – boo! Sometimes the gas or electricity meter reader calls. Sometimes it's someone wanting to see if the vicar is in and if he's in the mood to hand over the rail fare to Glasgow. On other occasions I simply gaze blankly for hours on end.

It's all work. Observing life, or gazing blankly, is what we writers do. It may *look* like idleness to the untrained eye, but when the eye is blank, the brain is working overtime.

My attic is painted pure white. Now and then I decide to change it to some other colour. I spend hours visualising how it will look and what new accessories I will need to buy, whether I will rearrange the furniture as well, or perhaps repaint the desk. Eventually I notice that I am in the grip of a displacement activity, and immediately resume my task of staring industriously out of the window. One of the good things about being a fiction writer is being able to imagine things vividly. I have imagined a series of different colour schemes very satisfactorily, without ever having had to pick up a paintbrush. I also repeatedly imagine that my study floor is covered with sea grass flooring, as all perfect studies are, and that there is a huge leafy palm that doesn't die of cold when I go away over Christmas, alas, leaving me feeling like a murderess.

The perfect cellar

A cellar can, broadly speaking, be treated like a loft. The main distinctions are that it is at the *bottom* of the house, not the top, and that it is *damp*. I'm talking about English cellars, here. The Germans

---

1. I once saw a lesser spotted woodpecker in the arboretum, and proudly told my son, adding, "They're quite rare. You don't often see them." To which he replied, "Durr. I *know*. That's why they're called *lesser spotted*."

manage to have dry cellars in which teenagers can have a bedroom, for instance; but in England even basements, which are basically cellars that are supposedly fit for living in, are damp.

The house I grew up in actually had a spring of water in the cellar, and in olden times this was the house's water supply, fetched up by means of a pump at the back of the house. This was pretty exciting. The house had been a pub at some stage, and at one side of the cellar was a strange trapdoor which opened onto a steep little grassy slope. This was where they used to roll down the beer barrels. Of course, being Baptists we didn't go in for any barrel rolling. Heck, we didn't even eat rum truffles. Mysteriously, though, even decades after the pub had been turned into a house there was still a beery smell about the place. It was the yeast spores in the atmosphere. According to my parents.

The perfect cellar, however, belonged to my Grandparents. They lived in an old Tudor house in Kent and ran a greengrocers shop. The cellar was used to store fruit and vegetables. I can still remember the smell, that unmistakable dark, earthy cellar-y smell mingling with the apples and onions. Many, many years later one of my sisters developed a pregnancy craving for this aroma and used to stand at the foot of her own cellar steps (listening to the flood water gurgle – what *is* it about English cellars?), breathing deeply for hours on end. I think this is the true explanation for the myth about pregnant women eating coal. It's just an excuse to go down to the cellar and snort the air.

The perfect wine cellar

I'm including this section because a VIK, helpfully reading through an early draft of this book, looked up at this point in astonishment and said, "Do you realise you've just written a section on the perfect cellar *without a single reference to wine*?" Well, you can tell *he* grew up an Anglican, that's all I can say.

Like the cupboard under the stairs, the wine cellar is a concept, not a literal place. We know people whose wine cellar – mind-bendingly! – is actually *in* the cupboard under the stairs. Our wine cellar is in an IKEA wine rack on top of the fridge. It currently contains

"*This idea of placing the wine cellar in the loft to discourage me from a stiff drink after the PCC meeting…*"

one bottle of fizzy grape juice and a bottle of Blue Nun.[2] I'd be the first to admit this does not constitute a perfect wine cellar. In an ideal world it would have lots of champagne and New Zealand *sauvignon blanc*. But hey, at least I don't use it to dry the baby socks on any more.

Thought for the day

Many people use their cellars and lofts as vast in-trays. It's not so much that they actively want to keep their obsolete computer, but that at the crucial moment, they can't make the decision about what to do with it. I'll just stick it in the loft until... you know, and then I'll.... Just for the time being. And there the computer will remain till you die or move house. There are sometimes things we do – good Christian things – that we've been doing for years without actually asking ourselves if we *actually want to do them*. Or even if we *need* to do them. Whole churches can get caught up in this, the doing of things because we've always done them, and can never quite find the right moment to look at the issue squarely and say "This thing, much-beloved, has served its useful function. Can we please get rid of it?"

---

2. Donated secretly by a mischievous parishioner during a vicarage garden party when I wasn't looking. I may give it to the bishop next time I'm asked round. He will just have to incline his mitre and pretend to be grateful.

CHAPTER 7
Housework

When I hear the word "housework" something in me shrivels up and dies. If I could afford to, I'd pay someone else to do it, even though that would involve tidying and cleaning the entire house every week in preparation for their visit. The main problem with housework is that it never stays done. And the most irksome thing of all is that the undoing of it is always undertaken by someone other than the doer. I suppose that tidying and untidying are separate gifts. We oughtn't to expect people to master both. It's just that we seem to have got the tidier to untidier ratio (i.e. 1:3) wrong here in the vicarage.

How to tidy

The basic rule is to start in one room, sort things into piles and STAY THERE until everything is sorted, THEN take the piles to their destinations. It's a simple time and motion matter. *Don't* pick up a paperclip in the kitchen and wander with it to the study, pick up a sock and take it upstairs, where you will see a dirty mug to bring down to the kitchen, etc. That is what idiots like me do.

Another approach is to trade: get someone else to tidy, saying you will vacuum and dust.

How to get teenagers to tidy their room

This cannot be done; or rather, it *can*, but like making rivers run up hill, it flies in the face of nature and takes a huge amount of energy and resources. The best way of tackling the problem is probably to shut the door and resolve never, ever to go in there, on the grounds that what you can't see won't annoy you. You will eventually lose all the drinking utensils in the house, however, as they find their way in to the pit never to emerge into the light of day again. At this point, ask your teenager (politely) if he or she would mind going out and buying some new mugs, using their own money. Unless they can think of an alternative solution to the cup crisis.

This may all be a bit too hands-off for you. Linking room tidiness to income is often recommended. Another more radical strategy is to issue a tidying ultimatum, after which any item not in its proper place will be tossed out of the window onto the lawn/street below.

But here's a thought. Parents can also stop doing chores. E.g.:

Teen: Mum, can you run me into town?
Mother: (wearily) I'll do it tomorrow.
Teen: But I need to go now!
Mother: I SAID I'd do it tomorrow, OK? Look, you're always on at me about driving you! That is so not fair! It's none of your business! It's my car, and I should be allowed to do what I like with it. None of the other parents have to! What is your PROBLEM here? Just get off my back, etc.

The quick tidy

This takes place when you get about three minutes warning of an impending visit. You will need to

- gather armfuls and run upstairs with them
- stack all paper neatly
- arrange items parallel/perpendicular to each other
- kick stray items under furniture
- spray polish into air

Remember: Never apologise. If they can sit down somewhere without getting food stuck to their trousers, it's tidy enough.

Laundry

When I was little we could always wind my mother up by singing "Rain, rain go away! Come again on washing day!" I now have "washing day" in the same category as French knitting using a bobbin with four nails banged in the top – i.e. in the childhood nostalgia box. Let's praise God for the automatic washing machine (first making sure our model is an energy efficient one and vowing never to do a half load).

Troubleshooting

Stains:

> Blood – pre-soak garment in *cold* water
> Tomato sauce – pre-soak garment in *warm* water
> Indelible marker – buy new garment

Wire from underwired bra wrecking machine – deny everything, pay bill, invest in one of those little nylon mesh bags for delicates.

Ironing

This should only be done when you actually need to wear something. Only slave through a basket of ironing if you (a) enjoy it, or (b) are in front of the TV using ironing as an excuse to watch the football. I occasionally like to indulge in a little recreational ironing of antique cotton pillowslips, but other than that, I've got it under control.

Things you shouldn't iron

- anything labelled drip-dry
- dusters
- anything belonging to another adult
- socks/underwear
- any part of your body

A note for Anglo-Catholics

Being High Church involves you with a lot of extra laundry, I'm afraid. All those purificators, chasubles, albs, altar frontals, etc. Still, "No pain, no gain", as it says in Leviticus.[1] Just one hint, though: never put underpants and altar linen in the same load.

---

1. Well, we Evos know it doesn't really, but Anglo-Catholics won't.

Vestments: the way forward

I've long been a fan of the idea of disposable (recyclable) plastic vestments. This would cut down on vicarage laundry and mean that the presiding vicar could relax during communion without worrying about how to lift wine stains from a white surplice. My other idea is to market disposable see-through plastic capes for bishops. This would allow them to keep their highly ornate vestments clean and dry while still offering lay people a chance to admire them.

Episcopal vestments often resemble furnishing fabric, so there is a danger that a large seated bishop might be mistaken for an armchair with protective covers on. And those white frills could be confused with antimacassars, couldn't they? But he could always fend people – actresses and the like – off with his crosier if they looked as if they were about to sit on him.

How to iron a shirt perfectly

Make sure the garment is slightly damp. And clean. Re-ironing a crumpled pre-worn shirt is a sluttish business, so don't even think about it. Set the iron to hot. Begin with the collar. If the shirt shrivels up and sticks to the iron, it is nylon, in which case, put it in the bin where it belongs. Next iron the yoke, followed by both sleeves. Then iron the main body, starting with the right front and working your way round. Then put it on, button it up and off you go. Return to house half an hour later and turn off the iron.

To iron an undergraduate shirt

Proceed as above, omitting all stages apart from the collar. Wear under a sweater.

Remember: Never iron in the nude.

Handy hint

How to put a cover on a king size duvet

People struggle with this, but it's actually quite simple. Turn your cover inside out. Burrow your hands inside until they reach the two far corners. With your hands still inside, grab two corners of your duvet. With a brisk flicking motion, shake them both. This will cleverly turn the cover almost entirely right side out onto the quilt. You can then tug the sides down into place and fasten it up. If you end up inside the cover, you are doing it wrong.

Dusting

This is an unhealthy obsession. Keep it to a minimum. Children brought up in sterile dust-free environments are far more likely to suffer from asthma.

Vacuuming

Issue advance warnings. After that, anything on the floor is dustbag fodder. Never point the nozzle at small children. They will be sucked up, and well they know it. Never try and remove blackheads with the upholstery tool.

Window-cleaning

This is cruel. Birds can't see clean windows and will fly into them.

CHAPTER 8
Gardens and gardening

*I*f you want to know what non-churchgoers do instead of going to the 10.30 service, the answer is, they go down to the local garden centre. In the C of E there are still those who are trapped between two worlds and who get up early to go to the 8 o'clock so that they've got religion out of the way and can go to the garden centre with a clear conscience.[1]

So, gardening is the new Christianity. People have their own private plot, which we might equate with the personal quiet time. They congregate once a week to worship at local garden centres. Many of them will make an annual pilgrimage to the Chelsea Flower Show, or some other horticultural jamboree, where they will hope to meet one of the great garden evangelists personally. They will go home generally revived and brimming with fresh creativity and enthusiasm to make the most of their gardens and be faithful in their daily walk with Alan Titchmarsh.

Some people tell me that among women of a certain age, gardening is also the new sex. A word of caution here: gardening is more work, takes longer and you get blisters. And it is not as happily combined with champagne. On the other hand, you don't often get to use a strimmer or edging tool in bed. Or to phrase it in the austere parlance of Christian Married Love manuals: "Jet washers and pesticides – these are seldom used."

The perfect garden

Let's define a garden as "an area given over to recreational land cultivation". Gardening may be jolly hard work, but it's recreational.

---

1. We call these people "8 o'clockers", which is a shorthand way of saying they prefer the Book of Common Prayer and the King James Version of the Bible, and will strenuously resist any attempts to get rid of the pews.

We aren't digging for victory these days, unless it's victory in the annual leek growing contest. We won't starve if we fail to put in our potatoes and carrots. We garden not because we must, but because we may.

I've come to the conclusion that the perception of what a garden is for has changed in the past twenty years. Gardens are now seen as an extension of the house, rather than an extension of the crop-growing land. Think of garden furniture, of the sudden proliferation of garden ornaments – fancy pots and sculptures, wall plaques, mirrors, wind chimes, ornamental water features. Think of the decking and fencing and the division of gardens into different room-like areas, with the little lawns or gravel patches like various floor coverings underfoot. Think of that outdoor kitchen – the barbeque.

The sense of the garden as part of your home is enhanced in many cases by a kind of border territory where garden and house merge; French windows which may be thrown open onto patios crowded with pots and planters, while inside there are more pots full of indoor plants, some of which go out in the summer, others of which resemble fair-sized trees. Or there are jungly conservatories, where you sort of sit outside under the sky, but not quite, and on clement days, may fling open the roof and doors and feel the breeze.

When I was little gardens still used to nod more in the direction of their farming origins. People grew rhubarb and fruit canes and apple trees. Flowers, though nice to look at, weren't simply ornamental. They might be destined for harvest festivals and flower shows. You certainly didn't put a sheet of heavy duty plastic over a perfectly good front lawn and cover it with granite chippings and plonk an urn in the middle because it was less bother.

The result of this is that a lot of us now feel vaguely ashamed of our perfectly good old-fashioned gardens. It is as though we have decorated our houses tastefully with the requisite expensive neutrals and antiques, but have perversely retained one room full of artexing and blown vinyl wallpaper. My advice is to hold your nerve. Old-fashioned gardens will be back and you won't have to rip out any decking and shovel up two tons of gravel to achieve the look.

How to have the perfect garden

You already know that I'm going to tell you to hire the perfect gardener, don't you? The thing with gardening is that it either takes a lot of time or a lot of money; frequently both. If you love doing it, fine. If you can think of better ways of getting a slipped disk, well, gardening is always going to be a chore. But hey, provided any lawns are kept fairly short (by somebody else), you can see large trees and beautiful flowers, ravishing scents waft on the breeze and you are lying in your hammock with a good book – well, things are pretty much perfect.

Weed killers

How to control weeds – this is a vexed area. Should we indulge in a spot of chemical warfare, or should we rely on sheer elbow grease? Is it ethical for Christians to use weed killer? This will have to be left to the individual conscience. There is, however, one highly effective home remedy for weeds, using an ordinary household substance, which I discovered quite accidentally.

Try this simple weed-eradicating experiment:

1. Walk about your garden noting where the biggest dandelions/patches of convolvulus are.
2. Go into the house and find an empty drinking utensil and fill it with a generous measure of wine or spirits.
3. Return to your garden. Carefully pour the contents of the glass down your throat and wait fifteen minutes.
4. Check the weeds. You will be unable to find them. NB. A second application may sometimes be required.[2]

Pesticides

I once wrote an article about slugs in the *Church of England Newspaper* and it produced quite the liveliest bout of correspondence in my time as columnist. Clearly slugs are something that Evangelical Anglicans feel strongly about, perhaps even more strongly than they feel about

---

2. If you cannot locate the garden, you have probably overdone it.

"Eeurgh! It's one of those smelly old beer traps.
I never go near them."

gay priests. Would attitude to slug disposal make a better acid test of orthodoxy, I wonder? Certainly Jesus had as much to say on the subject. But that is by the by. The consensus among the readership was that the best way to get rid of them (slugs, not gay priests, I hasten to add) was to put down so-called beer traps, into which the slug will fall and drown. It will be happy, but it will still drown. This is the Anglican way. Unfortunately, it will only get rid of English slugs. American slugs loathe warm beer and will slither straight past in quest of a nice bud[3] instead.

Well, I have never tried beer traps, I admit. But here is one way *not* to get rid of slugs from your garden. *Do not* shovel them up on a fish-slice and catapult them over the fence into your neighbours' garden. They won't like it. Neither the slug nor your neighbours.

Motto for the day

There is no such thing as a neglected garden, only a controlled environment for attracting seed-eating birds.

---

3. A good example of the classic So-Not-Funny adult pun I like to torment my sons with.

PART II
The perfect body

Introduction

We move now from the perfect home to the perfect body. In traditional Western thought this isn't too abrupt a transition, as we tend to view our bodies as little more than the home in which the *real* "us" happens to live. Just as the home of bricks and mortar (or clapboard and corrugated iron, if you live in New Zealand) can be improved and redecorated, so the home of flesh may be overhauled. Extensions may be built in the balcony area. Decayed and undesirable bits may be ripped out. This understanding of the human body is naturally highly desirable to the lucrative health and beauty market.

Better theologians than I have already pointed out the unbiblical nature of flesh/spirit dualism. My task here, however, is satirical, not theological. This means I get to poke fun at *you*, while *you* have to take it – or run the risk of looking like a humourless, self-important twit. That is the rule of satire. We satirists know no sacred cows. Apart from the inviolable position of satirists as social commentators and scourges of human foibles, of course.

CHAPTER 9
The perfect body

We live in a culture which is obsessed with youth and slimness. It's high time we had a simple no-nonsense guide to dieting. Here it is:

How to be perfectly slim

- eat less
- exercise more

Eternal youth

People may think they want to stay young, but it seems to me that they are a touch picky about which bits of youth they want to hang on to. How come nobody wants the acne, the exams and the conviction that everyone is staring at them? Wasn't that what youth was all about for most of us? But our society would have us think that it's youth we are all after, so let me guide you down this rutted path.

How to stay young

Staying young is not a matter of botoxing out your wrinkles. In any case, botox stops you frowning, and every sensible person knows that there are times when we need instant access to a good scowl. It is no use saying to children or incompetent road users, "Bear with me a few months until the botox has worn off and I will express my displeasure by frowning." The moment will have slipped by, gone forever.

Staying young is a matter of attitude. It is to do with a certain flexibility of mind and outlook. Don't fall into the trap of confusing "staying young" with "trying to imitate young people". *Don't* get your belly button pierced or your ankle tattooed. *Don't* wear teen fashions. *Don't* experiment with youth language. *Don't* learn how to send text messages. *Don't* try to dance like a young person. Well, unless your aim is to embarrass and mortify your children above and beyond the normal call of parental duty, that is.

Key attitudes to avoid

- I'm too tired
- I just need to lose a stone and then I'll *x* or *y*
- I'd feel stupid
- It probably won't work
- When you're my age you'll realise
- I could just do with a nice cup of tea

The age/paranoia equation

One of the interesting things I've noticed about getting older is that, yes, things begin to sag and wrinkle, but actually, you care less and less. The sorry paradox is that human beings are inflicted most acutely with paranoia about their bodies when they are at their most gorgeous. We might even be tempted to say that youth is wasted on the young. They don't appreciate it. They are too fixated on that single zit to realise they have the bloom, radiance and figure to distract a stained-glass saint. Honestly, these young slips of things thinking their size 10 bottoms are huge! Just wait a couple of decades, lovey, and I'll show you huge, we older women think.

My theory is this: acceptance of your body is inversely proportional to your youth/good looks.[1] Maybe this is because we become less exacting in our standards as we mature. We no longer expect our body to look like a film star's. We merely expect it to get us to the pub. I mean church. Sorry. Or maybe it's a question of looking in the mirror in an accepting way and saying, I look this way because I've smiled all those smiles, frowned all those frowns – wait, wait! I spot a mawkish little verse emerging here. Stand in front of your mirror every day (especially if you are a mother, or an American Bible Belt pastor's wife) and recite:

---

1. That's *conventional* good looks, in the worldly sense, of course. We Christians know that a person's worth is not determined by physical attractiveness, and that true beauty is an inward thing. Although we're certain Jesus wasn't short, fat and ugly with a massive conk and a receding hairline.

I've frowned all those frowns,
Smiled all those smiles,
Borne all those children,
Walked all those miles.
Hello body, old friend! I accept you!

(Then smack yourself briskly round the chops and knock back a big gin to take away the effect.)

Motto for the day

We cannot all be young and beautiful, but we can all be elegant.

Elegance

By elegance I do not mean a kind of glove-wearing prissiness that is forever worried about getting runs in its nylons. By elegance I mean flair, I mean style. Achieving style is not as hard as you might think. Here are some very simple pointers to help you.

1. Wear clothes that fit you, that suit you, and that you actually like. (Or, if you are a good sound Evangelical preacher, clothes that *fit* you, *fuit* you, and that you *fike*. I realise that neither "fuit" nor "fike" are genuine words, but how else will you grasp and remember what I am trying to say?)

2. Give to Oxfam all those clothes you are too fat for. (Or, for those of you in denial, that have mysteriously shrunk.) Yes, it's possible that you will shed those extra pounds and they will all fit again; but chuck 'em out anyway. What better way to reward your dieting achievement than buy splashing out on a new wardrobe? You will be able to tell yourself it's a good incentive. "Now I'll *have* to stay thin to justify the expense!" you say, as you sit down with your coffee and wodge of cake.

3. Avoid mixing patterns. Do not combine plaid and paisley, floral and stripes. Loud Hawaiian shirt, yes. Loud Hawaiian shirt with kilt, no. And for heaven's sake, loud Hawaiian *clerical* shirt, no, no and thrice no. Not with anything.

4. Co-ordinate. Do not wear red shoes with a blue outfit. In fact, do not wear red shoes.

5. Accessorise. The golden rule of accessories is: when in doubt, choose black. I've found time and again that the dullest of outfits may be transformed by the addition of a stylish broad-brimmed black hat, a fur stole, black kitten heels and a pair of dark sunglasses. Try it. People will stare at you and wonder if you are a film star. Unless you are male clergy, in which case people will assume you've got lost on the way to a tarts and vicars party.

6. Nail care. Nail varnish? Stupid stuff. Can't be doing with it, myself. And as for nail *extensions*! How do you pick your nose with those things on the end of your fingers, I'm wondering. If the good Lord had intended us to have long nails, he would never have given us teeth.

The Catherine Fox 3-stage nail care regime:

1. Look at nails.
2. Are they more than 3mm long?
3. If they are, clip or bite them back to 0.5mm.

Why? you ask. Because if you don't, the next time you do judo, they will get ripped off. I've learnt the hard way that to cry "Stop! Stop! I've broken a nail!" is to invite taunts from your fellow players, most of whom will be burly sweating blokes who never cry "Stop! Stop!" even if their *arm* has been ripped off.

Looking perfect on the beach

Women are obsessed with how they look, and nowhere more so than on the beach. How often do you hear a friend say, as if grimly resolving to climb Everest or reach the South Pole: "I'm going on a diet because I'm *determined* I'm going to wear a bikini in Crete."

Why? WHY? WHY?

Nobody feels relaxed in a bikini, either because they fear they are too old/fat, or because they are young and paranoid (see above). There are two reasons to wear a bikini: to show off your body and to get a tan. If you haven't got a tan, you can't show your body off. You can't get a tan without showing your body off. It's a Catch 22 situation. Or possibly Catch 42. Every way you look at it, it's a nightmare!

So why not stay off the beach, in the shade – in a nice terrace café, say – in cool linen clothes in a dramatic hat and dark glasses instead? Why do you *want* a tan?

Three good reasons to avoid a tan

tans
- give you wrinkles
- give you skin cancer
- are vulgar

Hair

Some of your important questions answered.

Q. How can I have Perfect Hair?
A. Pick up your credit card and go to a proper hairdresser.

Q. What can I do if I am going bald?
A. Get reconciled.

Q. Ought Charismatic Evangelical Christian women to dye their hair?
A. Irrelevant. They should have their heads covered.

Q. Are expensive hair products worth the money?
A. Yes, if you sincerely believe they are.

Sound hair advice for men

- Never drape.
- If a woman is happy with her hair, *your* life will be nicer.

CHAPTER 10
Health

The perfect doctor

I can speak with some confidence here, as I am a fully qualified doctor. Any emergency requiring a working knowledge of early Quaker eschatology, I'm your woman. Similarly, a VIK can legitimately elbow his way through a crowd – "Let me pass, please. I'm a doctor!" – in order to administer Calvin's missiology to the needy. The basic rule with doctorates is that they have to sound hopelessly – ludicrously – ivory towerish when someone asks you what you are studying. If you wouldn't actually prefer to answer "Oh, I'm just a housewife," then you are not studying for a proper PhD.[1]

The perfect home doctor

The Perfect Home Doctor is one you call for to visit you in your own home when you are too ill to go to your local surgery. Very occasionally you will experience a disorientating sense of déjà vu when the doctor appears. Don't worry, this is quite normal. All it means is that this is *your own GP*, not a visiting Jubba-Jubba doctor from the planet Zorgon employed by the deputising service.

In the olden days the perfect housewife was a bit of a doctor in her own right, able to apply fomentations, mix tinctures and lance

---

1. The same thing is true of being a novelist, incidentally. I've noticed that when hairdressers ask me what I do, I always have an urge to lie. They usually manage to ask when a general hush has fallen in the salon so that everyone will hear your bleated answer. And you know that the next question will be, "What kind of novels do you write? Are they romances?" (As in, "I can't help noticing you are a woman, so are they romances?") Then comes every writer's favourite: "Should I have heard of you?"

boils and so on. Perhaps, in this age when NHS resources are sadly overstretched, we need to rediscover some of the old home remedies.

Perfect home remedies

I have made use of the invaluable *Inquire Within Upon Everything* (1899 edition)[2] in an effort to bring you some sound advice. Quite frankly, there are so many illnesses and ailments the doughty housewife was expected to do battle with, that I cannot hope to include them all. Instead I shall explore a few that I hope may still be relevant to us today in the 21st century.

> **Cutaneous Eruptions.** The following mixture is very useful in all cutaneous eruptions: ipecacuanha wine, four drachms; flowers of sulphur, two drachms; tincture of cardamoms, one ounce. Mix: one teaspoon to be taken three times a day, in a wine-glassful of water.

(As with all home remedies I quote from this noble work, *Don't try this at home*.)

Now I think I'm right in saying that "cutaneous eruptions" are what our American friends call "zits". Picture your Victorian damsel in front of her mirror wailing: "Oh no! A cutaneous eruption! And it's the Hunt Ball tonight!" A friend of mine has a teenage son who suffers from the occasional cutaneous eruption. He asked her to buy him some fancy medicated spot-blitzing gel he'd seen advertised on TV. Her response was, "Let's try soap and water first, *shall* we?" – a bold innovative strategy for many teenage boys.

Some of you may be puzzling over the list of ingredients and terms occurring in the anti-zit recipe above.

Q. What is a drachm?
A. A drachm is *either* (Apothocary wt) 60 grains, i.e. 1/8 oz; *or* (Avoird.) 27 1/3 grains, i.e. 1/16oz. A grain, is, of course, 1/5760 of lb (Troy), or 1/7000 lb (Avoird.)

Q. What are "flowers of sulphur"?

---

2. Ninety-sixth edition, considerably enlarged and revised, London: Houlston and Sons 1899

A. I have no idea. Sublimed sulphur is laxative and diaphoretic, though.

Q. What is "ipecacuanha", and where can I get hold of some?
A. Ipecacuanha is a powerful emetic, i.e. vomit inducer. It is readily dispensed at any good hospital casualty department to bad mothers who have let their small children drink a bottle of baby paracetomol. It will act "well and easily", as my *Inquire Within* observes. In about 15 minutes your small child will be puking merrily on the floor, down your trouser leg, on the hospital bed, on him/herself – anywhere, in fact, except in the cardboard top hat specially provided by the nurse.

    Moral of this tale: Always screw the top on tightly.

Handy hint

If you are having difficulty opening a childproof lid, simply hand it to a bright six-year-old child.

> *Baldness when caused by Ill-health or Age.* Rub onions frequently on the part requiring it. The stimulating powers of this vegetable are of service in restoring the tone of the skin, and assisting the capillary vessels in sending forth new hair; but it is not infallible.

Give it a whirl! The great advantage of rubbing onions into your scalp is that people probably won't come close enough to see that you are thinning out. Garlic would be even better.

    Sadly, space does not permit me to enlighten you on the correct course of action in "APPARENT DEATH FROM DRUNKENNESS", "VIOLENT SHOCKS" and "FAINTING, HYSTERICS, &c" (Except to note that in the case of the latter, you should "avoid bustle and excessive sympathy".)

How to stay in perfect health

- never go into Health Food shops and read all the labels
- avoid all health publications/medical sections of papers
- eat your broccoli

How to have perfect skin

- stay out of the sun
- don't smoke
- select your ancestors with care

How to have perfect teeth

We English have a bad reputation in the States for our teeth. "English mouth" is what they call it. I'm in two minds. It's true that many English people have shocking teeth – crooked, chipped, decayed and tea-stained. But I almost, *almost* prefer that to what I call "American mouth" – teeth so perfect that they look false. Doesn't it seem a bit sad to you that American parents spend a fortune on dental results for their children that could be achieved far more cheaply by pulling the whole lot out and buying a set of dentures? No, let teeth have a bit of character, I say. By all means avoid decay and gum disease. Nothing wrong with that. But let's keep those pointy incisors, that quirky gap between the front teeth. So long as we aren't ashamed to smile, let's not worry too much.

CHAPTER 11
Fruit and vegetables

From the beginnings of time fruit has been associated with guilt. Without the role played by fruit, sin would not have entered Eden. These days we still catch faint echoes of that primeval guilt when we think of fruit – not because we have eaten it, rather the reverse: because we have *not eaten enough*. Anyone with small children knows that the best way of deterring them from doing something is to make it compulsory. Thou shalt eat five portions a day from the tree of knowledge! But we are not here to rewrite Genesis.

Children and fruit & veg

Perfect vegetables and how to prepare them for children

1. The oven chip. This remarkable vegetable grows in extremely cold inhospitable terrains, e.g. supermarket frozen foods sections, and can be recognised by its brightly coloured plastic outer shell. To prepare this vegetable, simply peel off the shell and remove handfuls which you will find come away readily in long thin strands. Alternatively, you can try shaking the opened shell over a baking tray. Some care is required here (postpone your evening sherry!) as the strands may all rush out together and fall all over the work surface and floor. If this happens, don't worry. Oven chips are virtually indestructible. Simply shovel them back in, along with any dog hairs and cake crumbs. (The heat of cooking will kill any germs.) The chips may then be baked in the oven until they look done. If they are left in the oven too long they become "Special brown extra-crunchy oven chips, yum yum! Look, Mummy's eating them! Well, bad luck, that's all there is." Serve with chicken nuggets, fish fingers or burgers. **Chef's hint:** put any leafy green vegetables you may have prepared straight in the bin. This is where they will end up, so let's cut out the middle man.

"What do you mean 'YUK'? You __LIKE__ this stuff!"

2. The tomato. This vegetable is unusual, in that it occurs only in liquid form. You will find some seedless varieties (e.g. ketchup) grow in plastic or glass bottles. Other seeded species grow in tins and have a different texture. The seeds come in all manner of shapes and sizes and this dictates the name given to the species, e.g. Batman, hoops, alphabet etc. (Sometimes the resemblance is a little fanciful.) You will find that small children love this vegetable for weeks at a time, before suddenly announcing that you *know* they hate it. Care must be taken on serving to ensure that the tomato doesn't touch any other food stuff, as this will render the meal inedible.

Perfect fruit and how to prepare it for children

1. Red. This versatile and useful fruit comes in many forms – jelly, jam, sweeties, yoghurts, biscuit middles etc. Many forms of red can be eaten raw. Simply strip off the outer layer of plastic and consume. Some types require diluting with hot water and leaving to set. Others may be eaten with a spoon or spread on bread. Any crusts should be discarded, as they make unwholesome eating. Brown bread should not be used, as it will spoil the delicate flavour of the fruit. One popular variety of red – the biscuit – is a bit fiddly to prepare, but well worth the effort. Pick off the crumbly top casing and scatter the crumbs on the floor. The fruit may then be gnawed off and the lower casing discarded down the back of the sofa cushions.

2. Blue. Blue fruit is sometimes known by its other name of "raspberries". These are edible only in their electric turquoise form which may be found in slushy drinks and fizzy pop.

Remember: children are not stupid. They are not fooled by bright colours. They know that carrots and sweetcorn are vegetables, even if they form part of a jolly smiley face on the plate.

Adults and fruit & veg

Here in the grown-up world, as I like to say to my children, we have a different attitude to vegetables. We actually enjoy eating them. Once we have shaken off the ghastly memory of school swede, that is. In the good old days vegetables were always boiled to within an inch of their lives. If you needed teeth to eat it, then, basically, it was undercooked. Here's some impeccable advice from my trusty 1899 *Inquire Within* on how to cook carrots:

> Some people place carrots into cold water, but this takes all the flavour out of them. They should be put into boiling water, with a little salt, and a piece of fat or dripping, and boiled for two hours.[1]

My view is that there is nothing wrong with carrots that a gentle frying in butter won't sort out. Cut them into thin strips first. Carrots may be eaten raw. In fact, even small children will eat raw carrots, especially if you say "Don't you dare eat those carrots! I'm going to cook them," and then turn your back for a few moments.

Perfect fruit moments

An absolute given with fruit, especially strawberries, is that they don't taste as good as they used to. In the case of strawberries this belief isn't just the work of the old rose-tinted rear view mirror; there is some factual basis for it. Strawberry growers, I very much fear, have fallen down to worship the idol Profit, not Quality, and tend to grow high yield varieties of strawberry, rather than those full of flavour. This is because people would rather have lots of cheap strawberries than a few nice ones. We get what we deserve. The other problem is that we can now get strawberries all year round, which tends to take the gloss off the experience. Winter strawberries are really nothing more than expensively packaged water.

The very best strawberries you will ever taste are wild ones picked from some sunny woodland bank, preferably one afternoon in childhood, and consumed on the spot. There will never be enough to make a pudding or jam, so cram them in as you pick them and savour that burst of intense strawberryness for one fleeting perfect moment.

---

1. See footnote 2, Chapter 10

Hints for getting the best out of imperfect strawberries

- choose local not imported
- if they aren't ripe, don't bother
- serve warmed by the sun[2]

Ripeness is all

All we ask from a fruit is that it be at the peak of its ripeness, and eaten in the right setting. For instance, there is such a thing as the perfect nectarine. I ate one in Normandy, once. It was a white nectarine, perfectly, exquisitely ripe, with the dark red colour around the stone bleeding dramatically into the pale flesh. I ate it with pongy French cheese and a glass of red wine after a meal with good friends around a farmhouse table with all the children finally asleep upstairs.

Ripe fruit is to be treasured. It is a rare find these days. You could wander the fruit aisle of your local supermarket for years without ever encountering something that was ready to eat. This is a little glimpse of hell – cold, sterile with the terrible knowledge that it could all be so different.

---

2. Or stick them in the microwave for ten seconds.

CHAPTER 12
The perfect cook

On being a domestic goddess

Not long ago a roofer's wife I know bought me a copy of Nigella Lawson's *How to be a Domestic Goddess*, evidently forgetting I ALREADY AM ONE. I *had* thought it was self-evident. In case there are others who are similarly ignorant, I shall now set the record straight by instructing you all on how to be perfect cooks. Let's start with something simple.

How to make perfect coffee

For many of you coffee-making is a stressful activity. You are trying to host a church meeting in your home, you have just kicked all the Lego hastily under the sofa, the children have just been banished upstairs to bed – despite the fact that they have only just remembered there's an important letter about football in their bag which *must* be dealt with immediately – and now, suddenly, there is a roomful of people expecting coffee. (**Chef's tip:** give up church meetings.) These are hardly the circumstances in which to construct the perfect coffee. Simply give them cheap instant. The perfect coffee takes time. It is a languorous and seductive process.

You will need, first of all, the best coffee you can buy from the church Traidcraft stall. Failing that, go to your nearest specialist coffee shop. Make your coffee. I personally like to use my proper stovetop espresso maker (£5 from Woollies sale) because it makes a nice noise and puffs the aroma of coffee through the house. A curate I know thinks this leaves the coffee tasting of aluminium, and there is room for many views here, no matter how wrong-headed.

If you are a real aficionado you can grind your own beans. This can be done quite easily in an electric coffee grinder, although a curate I know thinks that this can burn the beans and it's therefore better to spend 40 minutes laboriously grinding them in a hand-powered coffee mill in the sweat of your face. Well, that's up to you, of course. Go ahead if you've got the time. All I'm saying is, I'm quite happy with my OWN way of doing things.

If you wish you can keep your coffee beans (or ground coffee) in the freezer. This may, or may not, help retain its freshness. But honestly, if someone served you stale coffee, how would you ever know? It will, at any rate, keep it very cold, and ensure that your chicken nuggets have an authentic maccu picchu[1] flavour.

Next, microwave half an inch of milk in your Bodum milk-frother for 1 minute on full power. Full fat tastes nicer, skimmed froths better. Choices, choices! Pump the plunger approximately 50 times. You can use a battery driven frother, but you will lose the benefit of a brisk biceps work-out. Pour coffee into a proper cappuccino cup (available free from the Royal Shakespeare Company cafe, Stratford-upon-Avon, when the cafe staff are looking the other way), then gently add frothed milk. Sprinkle with drinking chocolate. Enjoy! At this point the phone will ring. Ignore it.

The perfect cappuccino cup

Always use the right kind of cup. Some manufacturers seem to think that cappuccino cups have straight sides. I know this, because they print the word "cappuccino" on them. Generally they print words on household goods because they think we are imbeciles and can't be trusted not to put underwear in the bread bin without written reminders. In this instance, however, I think it's part of a programme of disinformation, designed to brainwash us into thinking that cappuccino cups have straight sides, which they do not. Proper cappuccino cups are shaped like a shallow bowl with one handle. I hope this clears up any misunderstanding.

Let's move on now to the art of baking.

---

1. I notice that my computer doesn't recognise those words. This is probably because they are spelt wrong. It seems to be offering me "macaw pickup" as an alternative. Well, I suppose a strong jolt of coffee would perk most cage-birds up.

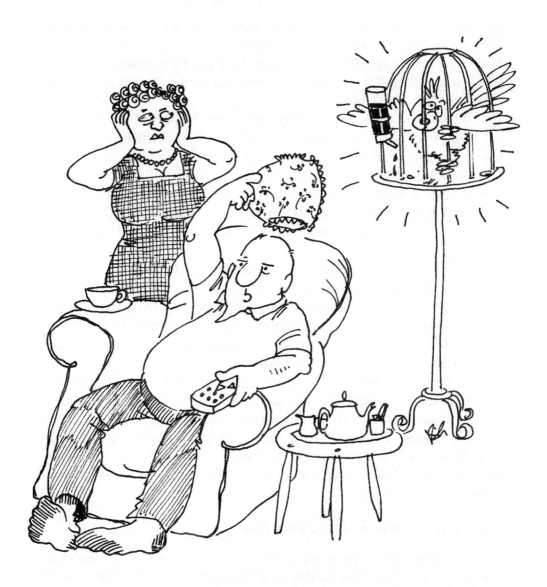

"*Try the tea-cosy, then we might get 5 minutes peace before it yells 'Milk and sugar Polly!'!*"

How to make the perfect sponge cake

The basic sponge recipe is the only known instance in the universe of something being improved by margarine. In every other single case Butter is Better. I think I'll just patent that phrase – unless, of course, I've just plagiarised it. Even in the case of sponge cakes, it only makes them *look*, not *taste*, better.

Now then. Ingredients. 150g soft marge, beaten with 150g castor sugar. If you beat it long enough it will go almost white, as will you, if you don't have an electric mixer. Beat in – one at a time – three eggs. Use the kind with white shells, as any bits that fall in by accident won't show as much. Then put your beater away. (**Chef's tip:** always turn it off before lifting it out of the mixture, or you will decorate your entire kitchen with uncooked cake dough splodges which encourages vermin.)

Next, weigh out 150g SR flour and sift it in. Stir in gently, then divide the mixture between two greased cake tins. There. GM 5 for 30 mins. I always add a teaspoon full of that very expensive vanilla essence.[2] When the cake is cool, sandwich it together with jam, butter icing (NB. there is no such thing as "margarine icing") or both, and sprinkle the top with sifted icing sugar.

When your cake is complete, give it away to someone less fortunate than yourself. You will find that this is a simple but effective way of cheering them up. I often bake things for people. In fact, I recently heard a VIK wandering about singing, to a well-known tune, "I'd like to bake the world a cake, and make it all OK." I think that was intended as a subtle rebuke for my belief in the soteriological power of baking.

Fat and sugar-free pavlova

This is a great favourite with dieters. Crack five medium-sized eggs into a bowl, putting the whites in a different bowl. (Put the yolks in the fridge and use them to make mayonnaise.) Be careful not to get any yolk in the whites mixture. We call this "separating the eggs".

---

2. A Baptist minister's wife I know tells me that you can make your own vanilla essence by adding vanilla pods to a small bottle of vodka. In their own quiet way these Baptists know how to have a good time.

This may seem obvious, but it is possible for a misunderstanding to arise here. Spacing the eggs out and putting them in different parts of the house won't give the same culinary results.

Make sure you put the egg whites in a *clean* bowl. This will prevent things like cobwebs and silver fish finding their way into the mixture and spoiling the final appearance of the pudding. Add a pinch of something (or a dash, if preferred) – I can't entirely remember what of (salt perhaps? vinegar? potassium chloride?) – anyway, it never seems to make a difference, so don't worry about it. Whisk the egg whites vigorously until stiff. Alternatively, get someone else to do it till they are stiff. Or use an electric mixer.

Next turn the oven on. You should have done this before starting, but again, it doesn't make any difference, so why worry? Turn it up to the right temperature. This is an interactive recipe, by the way. I have deliberately left some things for you to work out for yourself, like what Gas Mark to use. This should appeal to my male readers with their annoying problem-solving approach to life.

Next, get a baking tray and place a sheet of non-stick baking parchment on it. Draw a circle on it round a dinner plate. (Don't use wax crayon or lipstick.) Spoon the stiff egg white mixture on to the circle, pop it in the oven and bake till done. It will, of course, taste completely disgusting, as this is a recipe for mad health-conscious Californians, and not people like you and me. (**Chef's tip:** Why not try this simple alternative recipe? Ingredients: one frozen pavlova, available from most supermarkets. Method: defrost and eat.)

Lime chicken salad

You may occasionally find that the chicken you bought for Sunday lunch has quite a bit of meat still on it after the meal. This is certainly the case in the vicarage, as a VIK cannot stand up to our butcher, who is, admittedly, a consummate salesman. "A *small* chicken, please," says the VIK (consulting bossy list made by me). "We don't have any small ones today," replies the butcher. "I've got this 14lb turkey. Will that do?" And so the VIK comes home with a 14lb turkey. "That doesn't look like a small chicken," I complain. "Well, he said he didn't have any," comes the defensive reply.

So, if you have any meat left over, simply pull it all off the bones, chop it up and put it in a bowl. Next make a batch of fresh homemade mayonnaise. Don't be silly, of course you can. Just consult a recipe. Besides, how else are you going to use up all those yolks left over from the pavlova you've just made? Add the grated zest and juice of one lime then – here's the clever bit – get out that jar of hot lime pickle nobody likes and measure in about a teaspoon of the oil. Stir it, then mix with the chicken. Absentmindedly lick the teaspoon, then race up to Casualty to have your tongue dressed. The chicken carcase may then be put into a container and returned to the fridge with the intention of making a nourishing stock, then thrown out two weeks later. (**Chef's tip:** why wait? Put it straight in the bin now.)

Swan stuffed with peacock stuffed with lark's tongue paté in a black truffle Vicarage style

First, you will need a good-sized swan. Don't forget, you will have to get royal permission for this (or, if you live in a Roman Catholic country, a papal dispensation). The diocese of Durham, being historically a County Palatine, issues its own faculties for swan slaughter under the great seal of the Prince Bishop; which is terribly handy if you happen to be travelling in the North East. Or would be, had I not just invented that interesting historical nugget. You may like to substitute turkey for swan, if you enjoy eating putty with fibre glass in it.

Peacocks, on the other hand, are readily available at many National Trust properties. You will see them wandering about under cedar trees emitting their wailing cries. If you are quick, you may be able to cosh one over the head with your Thermos flask and wrap it in a picnic blanket. Failing that, ask your local butcher. He will say "We don't have any in today, but I have got this massive chunk of sirloin that could feed 25 starving cattle wranglers. It's very reasonably priced and perfect for a family of four. Will that do?"

Lark's tongue paté can be bought in any good delicatessen. To assemble the dish, simply put one ingredient inside the other – starting with the smallest – and stick it in the oven and cook it. This will allow all the wonderful aromatic, velvety, luscious, indulgent, pukka, succulent, lecherous, drooling and frankly sexual flavours to combine until you have to go and have a little lie down, and perhaps even smoke a post-culinary cigarette if you are that kind of person.

When it is ready, prepare your *jus*. (**Chef's hint:** If you haven't got access to some really nice black truffles, well, frankly I'm sorry for you.)

Faggots

Do you actually know what's in faggots? Do you even *want* to know? If you are vegetarian, or simply squeamish, look away now. According to my pre-BSE Mrs Beeton, they are made of "fry", which as far as I can make out is a euphemism for sweetbreads, which is a euphemism for the pancreas or thymus gland, which in turn is a euphemism for "gross yucky innard-y bits". You might also like to include heart, liver, lights and melts. My dictionary informs me that "lights" are lungs ("used in pet food"), but divulges nothing about melts. My opinion is that it means testicles. If you are better informed, well, good for you. Just don't bother writing in to tell me, as I shall continue to adhere to my own view, as befits a vicarage goddess.

To this medley of internal delights you may add "fat belly of pork", an onion, an egg, herbs of your own choosing (I know our butcher goes for curry spices when he makes his speciality award-winning "fag-a-loos") and *either* breadcrumbs or "caul fat", *or* –

No. Stop the madness. We all know we're not going to make this stuff. It reminds me of my brave yet misguided gastronomic adventure in Fontainebleau a couple of years back, when I chose something called *"andouillettes"* from a bistro menu. I say "misguided". Wilfully and deliberately misled, more like, by my fellow author who commended it to me as a regional speciality and informed me I'd like it. It proved to be a large pallid tube of semi-masticated offal which presented such an obscene appearance that I swiftly speared it with my fork while looking the other way. The menu had a mysterious number in brackets after the word *andouillettes*. Three, or four, perhaps. My companion later expressed the opinion that this referred to the number of people who had eaten it that year. He himself had steak. This just goes to show that you can never trust a novelist. They deal in fiction the way other people deal in facts.

PART III

Perfect relationships

"He's been taking this flying Bishop business very seriously ever since he went to see The Matrix."

Introduction

It is on the rock of human relationships that our efforts at perfection founder. Left to ourselves we can be pretty brilliant, frankly. Patient, kind, generous, forgiving – you name it. It's just that *other people* make it impossible for us. This is why monks and nuns laugh hollowly when outsiders suggest that living in community is an escape from the real world. There is nothing like being locked in a matrix of relationships for finding out the limits of your personal sanctity.

On the brighter side, a social matrix – whether it be marriage, family, friendships, religious orders, the work environment, the fellowship of believers – can also be the secure place in which you find out who you really are, the springboard for immense creativity. Always provided you don't go bonkers first.

CHAPTER 13
The perfect parent

How to be a perfect mother/father

A curate's wife I know has a badge which was given her by her sons. It reads "Not perfect, but still a star". I think this is probably the right idea, although I must confess that part of me thought my sons had better not buy *me* a badge like that. I want them to think I'm perfect, even though I know I'm not. In fact, I said as much to the curate's wife I know, and she quite rightly replied, "Oh no! I don't want them to think I'm perfect. I know I'll let them down."

There's a stage in your children's life when you are the best and the most beautiful Mummy/biggest strongest Daddy in the world. This is shortly before you become the most embarrassing being in the entire universe. I suppose there must be a brief window in which the balance is about right – the "Not perfect but still a star" stage. It's like the era between your tots waking you at some ungodly hour every morning, and the teen years when they only emerge from their reeking pit at 1pm. There must *be* a stage when it's perfect, it's just that you fail to recognise it until it's too late.

Motto

Perfection lies in the future or the past, never the present.

Thought for the day

Actually, that motto's not quite true. There will always be *moments* of perfection, when the glory that lies beneath the surface of our world will break through, flash momentarily, then fade. The art is spotting those moments when they happen along; or of trying to put yourself in the way of them. I can remember one example from when I was a child. I was running, running as fast as I could down our road, until I felt I could almost take off and leave the pavement and the village behind. I was running for no other reason than that I *could*, to express something inside me which made me feel that if I didn't run I would explode.

Funnily enough, these moments can occur against the bleakest of backdrops. When tragedy has struck and you are reeling with grief, along may come one perfect hour, in a perfect garden, with the sun and the scent of roses, and the turtledove's brooding call from the branches overhead, and the brilliant flash of a dragonfly over a still pond.

The thing to do with these moments afterwards is to keep them safe, not lament their passing. I like to take mine out now and then and turn them over in my mind. Being a shallow type of person, some of the top twenty moments in my treasure trove are to do with culinary perfection – that perfect little cream cake gobbled in a street in Venice in 1983 so I wouldn't have to share it with my fellow backpackers. That exquisite cappuccino drunk looking out over Scorching Bay in New Zealand one perfect summer morning. Well, actually dozens, no, *hundreds* of perfect cappuccinos drunk all over New Zealand. Why are we so useless at coffee in the UK?

Things the perfect mother avoids

- white clothes
- sharing expensive chocolates with small children
- treading barefoot on Lego
- swearing out loud
- falling over drunk in the playground
- refereeing pointless arguments
- instigating burping contests
- competing with other mothers

The art of competitive parenting

If you wish to engage in the art of competitive parenting you must be prepared quite ruthlessly to set your children's needs to one side. They may whine that they don't want to learn the piano, take up tennis, do Latin, join Brownies, be hot-housed for entrance exams, or have every spare moment of their lives timetabled to misery and only be allowed 30 seconds of TV/computer a day, and only then if it's educational. Take no notice! Remind yourself that it's all in a good cause.

Naturally, left to *ourselves* we would do none of those things. We wring our hands and hark back constantly to the golden days when it was possible to leave children to be children, growing up carefree and happy. It's just that *other parents* are so competitive. We don't want to be caught not doing the best for our children.

Useful throw-away lines for competitive parents

- "Of course, all mine could read before they went to school."
- "None of mine tasted chocolate till they were five."
- "We don't have a TV."
- "We're worried they aren't being sufficiently stretched."

How to stretch your children

This requires two adults, one holding the child's hands, the other the feet. On a count of three, the adults start to pull gently but firmly in opposite directions. Try to stop pulling before loud screaming/ dislocation occurs. Remember: no child likes being stretched. They would rather sit about all day eating junk food and playing computer games. But a wise parent ignores the objections and stretches the child for its own good.

Cooking for children: 3 golden rules

- no bits in
- no stuff on
- nothing touching anything else on the plate

Conflict in motherhood

I have been a mother for some twelve years now and I've noticed two interesting things. Firstly, that I am expected to know the whereabouts of every item in the house, regardless of whether it belongs to me, or I was the last to use it. Secondly, that something happens to your vocabulary during pregnancy. You lose all your nouns and never fully recover them. This results in *conflict*. E.g.:

Child: Mum? Mum! Where's my PE kit?
[Pause, while mother visualises where she last saw it.]
Mother: It's in the... behind the... you know, behind the, the thingy.
Child: What *thingy*?!
Mother: Oh, the *thingy* thingy. Behind the wotsit in the... you know.
Child: (getting desperate) No, I don't know! WHICH THINGY? I'm going to be late for school!
Mother: (seeing a way out) Listen, *you're* responsible for your PE kit, mate. I can't spend my whole time etc. etc. I suppose I'm going to have to get up and look for it myself, am I?
Child: Well, I left it by the washing machine. You SAID you'd wash it and you HAVEN'T and now I'm going to be late for school AND IT'S ALL YOUR FAULT! Oh, hang on, here it is, behind the kitchen door. Thanks Mum, bye!
Mother: (rolls eyes) See? Just where I said it was.

How to avoid guilt

You can't. In my experience, either s/he will be the only child who has taken in a Christmas present for the teacher, or the only child who has not. And either way it will be your fault.

The role of the perfect father

The father's role in the family is to demonstrate that there is an alternative way of being human in this world. Children pick up on this very quickly. If the mother snaps "Don't say that!" the child soon learns to respond, "*Daddy* says it." I'm afraid the differences between mothers and fathers tend to fall out rather predictably along gender stereotype lines. The mother tries to make the world a safe and secure place for her little ones. The father throws them up into the air after they've eaten a big meal, or pretends to toss them off high buildings or into the sea.

In the vicarage we have a division of labour when it comes to teaching our sons. It is a VIK who patiently imparts specific skills, such as learning to read, or ride a bike, or tell the time. I find I can spend approximately three seconds trying to teach a small person to tie their shoelaces before I shout in exasperation, "Oh let me, for heaven's sake!" But when it comes to long-term open-ended teaching, like how to appreciate the world of nature, or be a good person, that's when I come into my own. "Be kind, be nice, oh look! a baby duckling! don't throw sticks at him! listen, a willow warbler! gently!" etc.

Bringing up sons

There comes a point when a mother has done the major part of her role in bringing up sons – though boys never stop needing their mother at some level, for emotional security perhaps, and laundry services. I can teach my sons many things, including, I hope, how to be a good (if not perfect) person. But I can't really teach them how to be men. I can teach them what kind of man *I'd* like them to be, but that's different. Basically, I'm stumped, because I have no idea what it feels like to be a thirteen-year-old boy. I gather it's a bit like pootling along quite happily on your push bike, when all of a sudden someone claps a 750cc engine onto it. What a lad needs is a reassuring presence to show him what to do with all this raw power; someone who understands that willow warblers and baby ducklings and being nice are all very well in their way, but not quite where it's at, somehow. And the more blokes about the place to show him it's basically OK, the better.

Bringing up daughters

When it comes to girls, well, I know what it's like to *be* a daughter, even if I don't *have* any. Once the daughter is in her teens the mother's role is to know nothing about anything, to totally, totally, like not understand, to be so not fair about everything, and basically ruin the poor girl's life. That may sound like a tall order, but don't worry about how you will achieve all this. It will happen automatically, regardless of how you behave. The only consolation for you, while the mobile

"Verity's signed up for a day release course with
the Foreign Legion — naturally I'm discouraging her."

phone/skirt length/boyfriend wars rage, is that everyone else will compliment you on how charming, intelligent and considerate your daughter is and what a credit to you.

What to do with fifteen-year-old girls

My suggestion, based on my observation that daughters are only truly vile to their mothers, is for mothers to organise themselves into syndicates and arrange a monthly daughter swap. I suspect that most girls will keep decent hours, do their homework and tidy up quite cheerfully for a few days at a time in someone else's house. And most mothers will be able to refrain from criticising another woman's daughter's make-up/diet/clothes. This will give both mothers and daughters a well-earned break from one another.

Some pointers on being the perfect grandparent

- bring sweets/money
- sing songs
- read same story fifteen times or as required
- arrange trips to zoo/swimming pool/cinema
- accept offers of "help" while cooking
- play endless games of Monopoly/cricket/football
- be interested in computer games/football stickers
- believe tall tales
- never say "Not now" or "We'll see"

CHAPTER 14
Perfect spousehood

Clergy spouses

"Clergy spouse" is the rather inelegant term used by the Church of England instead of "vicar's wife", because these days it is possible that the vicar's wife is a bloke. In this chapter I will be examining what goes to make up the perfect vicar's/minister's spouse. By which I do not mean "the spouse of the perfect vicar", since we all know that the perfect vicar doesn't exist. Well, not until he or she has left the parish and the new priest needs taking down a peg or two. Once clergy have moved on they retrospectively acquire all manner of skills they were widely known to lack during their time in the parish. These will begin to manifest themselves about two years after leaving, when the new pastor's honeymoon period is over. So the message here to ministers is: move on every two years and you will never go out of favour.

The perfect clergy spouse

The perfect clergy spouse needs to be perfect in his or her own right. Oh, let's forget all this tiresome his-or-her business, shall we? Most ministers are men, most ministers' spouses are women. I will therefore adopt the generic "she" to describe the pastor's spouse and not worry unduly about the sensibilities of prickly masculinist clergy husbands. Every sensible person, I'm sure, accepts that men are included in the generic "she"; and that when I talk about the perfect vicar's wife doing the flowers, baking scones, wearing 1980s Laura Ashley frocks and giving birth to clergy children, we all understand that this *equally* applies to *men*. Honestly, I get so fed up with this inclusive language nonsense, don't you?

I think it will be useful to break the perfect vicar's wife down into manageable chunks, the better to understand her various roles. We will adopt the traditional categories of *physical*, *spiritual* and *culinary*.

The physical appearance of the perfect vicar's wife

There is no fixed ideal of body type for the perfect vicar's wife. The only important thing is that you look and feel uncomfortable with yourself. This will give off the message that you know your body is sinful. An easy way to achieve this is to wear clothes you don't really like and which don't actually suit, or even fit you. Too tight, too baggy – either will do. Go for a look which is about ten to twelve years out of date. Pale tights with sensible shoes works well. Make sure you get your skirt length wrong. Avoid hairdressers. Above all, you've got to give off the message that you are starved of light, struggling to survive in the shadow of your husband's Important Ministry, that you don't really know who you are, what the point of *you* is. You must be very, very angry, but never able to express it. Goodness, no! You must turn this anger inwards and become depressed.

Is this a bit near the bone? Is it annoying you? Channel that anger inwards! Listen to those voices telling you you're useless. Try feebly to reassure yourself that outward appearances aren't important, it's what's on the inside that counts. Then realise in despair that there's nothing very exciting going on *inside*, either. You are a miserable failure.

Et voilà! The perfect stereotype of the clergy wife.

Clergy wife motto for the day:

"Stuff the lot of you, I'm going to do what I want."

Write these words on a piece of paper (or work them in cross-stitch, if you prefer) and contemplate them each day before breakfast. I suggest this not because I feel the world or the church would be a better place if it were peopled with bolshie vicars' wives sticking two fingers up at life, but because your job is to be the best you can be. If you don't do that job, it ain't gonna get done.

Don't automatically assume that if you want to do something, it must therefore be unacceptable to God. It *may* be unacceptable to some of the congregation, but that's what we refer to in the trade as "TP" – *their problem*. One of the most constructive days of my life was when it occurred to me that God might actually want me to do the thing I most enjoyed, i.e. write fiction. And believe me, I have had some very narky letters from fellow believers who find my fiction, I believe the word is, "*unhelpful*".[1] Work out your own salvation in fear and trembling, as the Good Book says. Don't agonise over how you think other people think you should be working your salvation out.

How to dress

Exactly as you like. Provided you really do like it, that will be perfect. I went through a stage of wearing Doc Martens, which at the time were slightly scary and radical. Sadly, they have now become *de rigueur* for a certain type of young(ish) clergy wife – indeed, are well on the way to becoming the new navy blue open-toed sandal with American tan tights – so I now eschew them, with a languid "Oh, that is so 90s." These days I mostly wear kitten heels.[2]

The perfectly spiritual vicar's wife

In the olden days of crimplene and pack-away plastic rainhoods to protect your hair-do, there were a great many spiritual roles for the vicar's wife to fulfil. She was expected to run the Mothers' Union and/or the Sunday School. Naturally, she was also expected to attend church every Sunday. The vicarage was not a private home. It was an extension of the church building, and as such, parishioners expected to have the run of it for holding meetings and running working parties to sew fancy goods for the bazaar. While it was assumed she prayed and so on herself, the main spiritual function of the vicar's wife was to ensure that NOTHING CAME BETWEEN HER HUSBAND AND HIS MINISTRY. This included children. If the vicar was in his study, the vicar's wife's job was to ensure that the children didn't disturb him as he prepared his sermon, or wrestled like Jacob with the

---

1. Happily, most of them turn out to have implausibly silly surnames. And there is always the possibility of writing them in to my next work and giving them prolapsed piles.

2. This is what we refer to in the trade as "AFL" – a fat lie. I occasionally wear kitten heels if I am going out somewhere posh, and only then if I know I won't have to walk more than 50 yards.

"Sure they _look_ cute but you can't catch mice in them, can you?"

Lord. Or read the sports pages or had a nap. There are grown-up clergy children today from that era whose abiding image of fatherhood is a shut study door.

Time marches on. These days, in order to be perfect, all you have to do, really, is turn up for Sunday Services. If your predecessor's wife never darkened the church doorway, so much the better. The parishioners will be grateful to you just for being a churchgoer. They may get a bit cheeky and push their luck and ask if you would like to help with the Sunday School, but smile and say firmly, "I never do that." (Unless you really *want* to help with the Sunday School, of course, then by all means say yes.) Never explain. Never apologise.

Useful platitude

Nobody expects a GP's wife to hold asthma clinics.

The culinary skills of the perfect vicar's wife

In a more genteel age it was expected that the vicar's wife would be able to make a cucumber sandwich so thin you could read Evensong through it. If you find yourself in a church where this is still expected, try making one so thin you can read the job adverts in the back of the *Church of England Newspaper*, and find yourself a new parish. (**Chef's hint:** If you can't slice it thin enough, poke a hole through.)

I assume that this – coupled with twin-set and sensible shoes – is what people have in mind when they ask me if I am a "traditional vicar's wife". To which I reply, "I'll just go and pop the urn on."

CHAPTER 15
The perfect Christian

I suppose no book on personal perfection for the Christian market would be complete without a chapter on how to be a poerfect Chritsian. As you can see, I am far from being a perfect typist, even, let alone a perfect disciple; but I will have a stab at it.

The perfect Evangelical Christian – your checklist

- correct stance on homosexuality
- smile
- guitar
- daily Quiet Time
- T-shirt with proselytising slogan
- big Bible
- short accounts with God
- headscarf (female)
- ego (male)
- children (if married) with biblical names
- ability to just really split infinitives
- tongues (Charismatic)

The perfect spiritual adolescence

When I was in my early teens it was quite clear to me what being a perfect Christian entailed. Firstly, you needed to be male. Secondly, good looking. Thirdly, under 40. You had to speak with great authority the words given you by the Holy Spirit. Spiritual gifts were essential – healing, miracles, speaking in tongues, prophecy, words of knowledge. In short, to be a perfect Christian you needed to be God's Man for Our Time; a doughty warrior in the spiritual battle, a mighty evangelist, with an Important Ministry. And it helped if you had your own car so that I didn't have to rely on Dad for lifts.

One thing that wasn't required, as far as I could see, was any rigorous intellectual effort. The whole armour of God did not seem to include a thinking cap. Theological College was a place you went to in order to lose your faith. The crucial thing was to maintain a moment-by-moment communication with Jesus. Mere human intelligence and common sense were stumbling blocks and snares of the Evil One. The more ludicrous the thing you thought the Spirit was prompting you to do, the more likely it was to be genuine.

No detail of your life was too trivial for God's concern. Not sure which jeans to wear? Ask Jesus. Should you make a cup of tea? Take it to the Lord in prayer. It was possible that God was wanting you to make a cup of tea because – unbeknown to you – a suicidal ex-convict with a heroin habit was at that very moment stumbling up to your door, about to ring the bell and ask for a cup of tea, and to cut a long story short, they would be converted, healed and come off heroin and their story would be told in a best-selling Christian paperback. And all because you sought the Lord's will over making that cup of tea!

The one thing that the perfect Christian life should never be was boring. You had to be in a permanent state of excitement about your faith and the Lord. Your testimony was supposed to be strewn with mini-miracles and "so-called" (sneer) "coincidences". I assumed that maturing as a Christian meant making fewer and fewer mistakes, falling less often into the same old sins, and accumulating more and more of the answers.

But hey, that was my teens. I'm sure it had as much to do with my age as the theology I embraced. I don't regret my Christian Youth Fellowship Hunt-the-Blessing years. You are *meant* to be passionate and radical at that age. It only dawns on you slowly that instead of getting more and more answers you are in fact getting more and more questions, and that perhaps the best you can hope for is a filing system comprehensive enough to store them in.

How to annoy Charismatics

One very good way is to do what I have just done – suggest that Charismatic experience is merely an immature phase you go through as a Christian. As an undergraduate I was once sternly ticked off by a pastor for no longer using my gift of speaking in tongues. He said it was ungrateful of me and God was wanting me to really get down and repent, as it was like being given a present and instead of using it, just putting it on the mantelpiece and forgetting about it.

Yes, *but*, I thought afterwards, when the moment for saying it had slipped by (the story of my life – all those brilliant ripostes thought up two days too late), I was given a doll's cot when I was a child and I don't think it's ungrateful of me not to play with it at the age of 19.

And another thing, (I also didn't think of saying), why is nobody concerned with my not using the *brain* God gave me, the thing that, above all others, makes me *me*? It strikes me that this would be the biggest ingratitude of all.

What would Jesus do?

This can be a useful rule of thumb when we find ourselves facing a dilemma. I've seen the abbreviated form – WWJD? – on a yoyo. The yoyo didn't work properly, so I was left wondering whether the answer was, He'd buy a better yoyo. But setting yoyos reverently aside for a moment, let's ask ourselves what Jesus has to say on the subject of being perfect.

One thing that we must immediately conclude from the life of Jesus is that being perfect does not entail being successful. Dismiss the idea of worldly wealth being an infallible sign of God's blessing. I spit upon the Prosperity Gospel. In love, of course. When I was growing up people used to chide gently that Christians should never say they were "All right *under the circumstances*". No, no! Christians were supposed to be *over* the circumstances. I have one word to say to that: Gethsemane. I think it's safe to state that the Gospel writers wish us to understand that things were, you know, *getting* to Jesus a bit there.

Happily for me, Jesus provides us with a nice sound bite on the subject of perfection: "You must be perfect, as your heavenly father is perfect." Matthew 5:48 (RSV).

Christian perfection

A brief scan of the Bible commentaries belonging to a VIK reveals that most scholars (while being hopelessly off the rails and well on the slippery slope to atheism) are of the opinion that Jesus wasn't talking about moral perfection here. He wasn't setting up a ridiculously high standard in order to reduce us to despair; a kind of spiritual equivalent of "Ye shall have the thighs of a supermodel," or "Ye must kick even as Johnny Wilkinson."[1] No, we are supposed to imitate the character, the ways of God, not struggle in vain to reproduce his works. The context is Jesus telling us to forgive our enemies and pray for those who persecute us. In this way we will be children of our father who is in heaven who "makes his sun rise on the evil and on the good".

It's a bit like families. When someone says to my son "You are just like your father," they don't mean he's a vicar, can drive a car, and read Calvin's commentaries in Latin without falling asleep. They mean that they've spotted a family resemblance. A VIK is one of life's enthusiasts. Our sons are the same. Witness the following little exchange:

> **Son 1:** Hey! It's wombats on the telly! Wombats!
> **Son 2:** Wombats! Cool!
> **Son 1:** (after a pause) Do you know what wombats are?
> **Son 2:** No.
> **Son 1:** (portentously) They're bats that wom.

I think I'd sum up the idea of being perfect the way God is perfect like this: it's an impartial open-hearted generosity to one and all.

---

1. And he is welcome to come and practise taking penalties in my garden any time. If he breaks someone's greenhouse, I'll be safe, because it will be at least a quarter of a mile away.

CHAPTER 16
Behaving perfectly

How to have revenge

Behaving perfectly is the best revenge, people tell me. This is quite helpful for the Christian, as most other forms of revenge – from giving a tell-tale a Chinese burn to tipping paint stripper on an erring husband's sports car – are precluded by the Scriptures. Vengeance is mine, saith the Lord, I will repay. Do good to your enemies. Love those who persecute you. When your enemy is hungry, feed him. All these things are forms of behaving well, and the Bible acknowledges that there is an element of revenge here: "In doing so you will heap burning coals on his head." Perfect behaviour is a way of capturing the moral high ground; indeed, of building a luxury home there, and sitting on the decking in a comfy lounger with a nice cold drink admiring the view. In other words, as my wise old Mum always used to say, *Don't sink to their level.*

In the Gospels Jesus admonishes us to turn the other cheek when someone slaps us. At first glance this sounds like we're being told to become doormats – dignified Christ-like doormats, but doormats nonetheless. But scholars have pointed out that turning the other cheek is not as passive as it might at first seem.[1] "If someone strikes you on the right cheek," Jesus begins by saying, "offer them your left as well." Given that most people are right-handed, a blow to the right cheek is going to be a contemptuous backhander, dished out by someone to a social inferior. By offering your left cheek as well you are implicitly challenging the striker. Now do it again, but this time

---

1. This is why we read Bible commentaries. It's surprising what you can learn from people whose faith has been totally destroyed by studying academic theology.

treat me with dignity. Abuse me if you will, but take me seriously as a fellow human being.

How to cope when the wicked prosper

Read Psalm 37

Perfect manners[2]

In themselves manners are a mere airy nonsense. Your human worth is not decided by whether you hold your knife like a pen or drink the finger bowl. Etiquette varies from culture to culture. For example, in some countries it is considered polite to let fly with a massive belch to signify your appreciation of a good meal. Sadly, some may think, this is not the case in the West, even if you are an extremely talented belcher and can burp the phrase "Thank you for my lovely tea, please may I get down?" True good manners are all to do with consideration of others. They are to do with making others feel comfortable and welcome.

Most of us have a fairly good sense of what is socially acceptable in the culture in which we live. Only occasionally do we hit upon a social dilemma that leaves us flummoxed. Our weekend newspapers carry columns devoted to answering this kind of question. There are some highly specialised problems which come the way of clergy and other practising Christians, though, and I have ransacked my mailbag to find some instructive examples for you to ponder.

Manners for the modern minister

Dear Ms Fox,
I am a vicar in the Church of England and recently found myself in a sauna with a couple of other men after a squash match. One of them began regaling the other with a detailed account of a dirty weekend, not knowing I was a clergyman. Ought I to have said something at the time? As it was, they saw me getting dressed afterwards and realised, and were covered with embarrassment.
Yours sincerely,
Rev A. Non.

---

2. This will be dealt with more fully in the following chapter.

Dear Mr Non
Always wear your dog collar into the sauna.

Dear Ms Fox,
While visiting a retirement home recently, I was sitting and chatting
to a very pleasant elderly woman. While she was talking her false
teeth suddenly slipped. Luckily she caught them and put them back in.
However, if she hadn't, the trajectory would have carried them straight
into my crotch. What would be the etiquette there? Should I hand
them back, or let her pick them up herself?
Worried of St Wilfred's

Dear Worried,
Never sit down in a retirement home.

Dear Ms Fox,
I belong to an Independent Evangelical Fellowship, but I sometimes
visit Anglican churches. I get confused in the bit called "The Peace".
Can you explain what it is, and what I am supposed to say and do?
Just really yours in His Love.

Dear Mr/Ms Just-Really,
Officially, "The Peace" is the point in the Eucharist (Lord's
Supper) when we greet one another in the name of Christ,
usually by shaking the hand of those around us and saying
something like "Peace be with you". In some churches, though,
Christ's peace is expressed by staring steadfastly in front of you
and hurrying on to the next hymn. In other congregations the
Peace is a lengthy opportunity to spread gossip and/or viruses.
Take note of what those around you are doing and copy them.
Basically, a simple handshake should suffice, unless you spot
someone incredibly good-looking, in which case it's fine to cross
over to them and give them a hug and a Christian kiss.

How to overcome shyness

This is one occasion when I am not going to advocate opening a bottle
of champagne. Bracing yourself with a quick sherry before social

encounters strikes me as setting a very dangerous precedent. I can remember being strangled by self-consciousness in my early teens. I hesitate to say I was *shy*, because people who knew me back then will probably read this book and denounce me as a liar. But I can remember a stage when I found it almost impossible to read out loud. I used to get all tangled up and go bright red. In fact, when I was thirteen my most often repeated petition to the Lord (apart from please to postpone the Second Coming until I was properly converted) was that I would get through the day without blushing. Blushing was an ordeal because there was generally someone around – a sister or a "friend" – who would point out my embarrassment and focus the attention of the entire room on it.

Eventually most of us realise that by and large other people neither notice nor care if we have blundered and feel a twit in some social setting. And if they *do* care, why, they are not nice kind people and we can safely set their opinion to one side. One of my sisters always used to say that if she found someone intimidating – old battle-axe teachers and so on – she used to imagine them sitting on the loo.

Etiquette on the road

This is helpfully articulated in something we refer to as "The Highway Code". If you follow this you won't go far wrong. There are, however, refinements you might like to work on. Letting people out of side roads is an obvious one, or flashing someone coming the other way to let them go through a partially obstructed bit of road ahead of you. Don't try this in France, though, where flashing your lights means the opposite, i.e. Outta my way, sucker – I'm coming through!

Bloke driving – the etiquette

- reach for barrier tickets through car window, never open door
- clench barrier ticket in teeth
- drive round car park 14 times searching for space nearest shop
- overtake wherever possible
- lane hop in traffic jams
- never fasten seatbelt until car has reached 30mph
- never stop car to remove sweater

"As always with literal interpretation it can be taken to unhelpful extremes."

- set out confidently for destination leaving directions at home
- navigate by the sun
- collide with other vehicles head on at high speed

Useful catchphrases

- In your own time, love
- Come on, come on!
- Yeah, you too, mate.
- Moron!
- ****! Never mind. It probably hasn't got any film in

Girlie driving – the etiquette

- park in first available place, however distant from destination
- when parking *either* leave at least one wheel on pavement *or* straddle two bays
- plan route to avoid right turns
- stay behind slow vehicles for 20 miles
- stop car two metres from ticket barrier, fail to reach ticket through window, open door, reach, fail again, get out of car, snatch ticket, lurch through before barrier slams on car roof
- collide with stationary objects at low speed
- navigate by landmarks (e.g. shops)
- learn route and stick to it forever
- map read correctly only while travelling north

Useful catchphrases

- Where am I going now?
- Are they honking at me?
- Is this a one-way street?
- Oh look! That's the new shop that –
- Sorry!

CHAPTER 17
Perfect manners

When I was a girl people were forever telling me to behave like a little lady. This meant things like wearing a nice frock and not gobbing on people's heads from upstairs windows. It was pretty clear to me from a very young age that there wasn't much mileage in ladylike-ness. Being a boy, it seemed to me, was much more fun. Boys, everyone said excusingly, would be boys. Nobody expected *them* to wear frocks. And gobbing was practically compulsory for boys. To this day I find I still can't spit creditably. When I'm out running, this is; not during prayer meetings or anything. Your average bloke can hawk several feet – indeed, you can't be in a Premiership football team unless you can gob accurately at the ref's feet from ten paces; but I always seem to end up flobbing down my front. That is what patriarchal society does to us.

In this chapter I will examine various wise maxims handed down from generation to generation, to see if they still hold good today.

Age before beauty

This is one of those annoying and pert things that younger women are occasionally unwise enough to say to me. There are several ripostes. "Grace before meat" was the one my mother used. "Pearls before swine" has a nice biblical ring. "Leg before wicket" will leave them wondering if this is a rude joke they don't get. Failing all else, incline your head graciously as if implying you will pretend you didn't hear that crass remark. As I'm always saying to my sons: Take no notice. They always feel this is too passive. I once saw the younger one thrusting his face into his older brother's and bellowing "NO NOTICE!"

But in general, I believe courtesy requires us to defer to our elders. The older I get, the more I am convinced of the wisdom of this.

Ladies first

I get the impression that many men these days no longer know if they should open doors for women. Personally, I'm never offended by what I take to be courtesy on the part of another person. Thank you notes, bunches of flowers, expensive chocolates – these are always welcome. I can't imagine looking daggers at some nice gent who has offered me a seat. There are still gender inequalities to be righted, but I don't see Britain's bus service as the appropriate forum.

It's all to do with whether we feel patronised. And this is where the lines get blurred and a poor chap doesn't know where he is. Personally, I wouldn't feel at all patronised if an unreconstructed string-vest chauvinist said "Look, love, shall I park that for you?" I would hand over my keys with gratitude, because my sense of self-worth is not bound up in my parallel parking skills. The suggestion that I needn't bother my fluffy head with being clever is different.

But to return to public transport. I always teach my children – as my mother taught me – that you let people (regardless of gender) coming *out* of buses and buildings through the door first; and that younger people defer to older people in these matters. Barrelling old ladies aside is not polite. Some of them deserve it, but we try to exercise self-control.

Children should be seen and not heard

This is a piece of Victorian rubbish. If children were not audible we would be deprived of a vital source of merriment. I once overheard a small girl being shushed by her parents during a communion service. "But I get ANNOYED in church!" she bellowed, voicing the mood of half the adults present, I suspect.

Children should be taught not to interrupt, though. Eventually they learn not to barge into adult conversations with loud requests and complaints. Instead they fidget on the sidelines going "Mum. Mu-u-um!" *sotto voce*, until in the end you turn in your gracious maternal way and shout "WHAT?!"

Possibly the best way of teaching children not to interrupt is to make sure *you* don't interrupt *them* when they are telling you important stuff about having got to level eight on their *Yawn Master*,

Oracle of Boredom game. If you find this difficult – and it is difficult – then you will have some insight into what it is like to be eight, and trying to have a quiet word with your Mum about needing a second Mars Bar while she and her friend are droning on and on about the new IKEA catalogue.

Don't talk with your mouth full

The fact is, you *cannot* talk with your mouth full. A good friend of mine[1] once got an entire orange jammed in her mouth[2], and believe me, she uttered not one word for several anxious minutes. It's possible to talk with your mouth *half* full, and most people do it occasionally; especially if the phone rings halfway through a meal. When this happens you have to leap to your feet and lunge for the phone as if a war siren has just gone off and the house is about to be hit by a cruise missile. If you are stupid and haven't heard of answer machines, that is.

Don't eat with your mouth open

Now this one I agree with. My sons sometimes test to see if I have changed my mind by coming up close to my ear and chomping a banana in a loud disgusting way. They generally do this when I am reading a book, which is fortunate, as it provides me with a handy whacking tool without making me get up out of my chair to find one.

A gentleman always walks on the right

I've heard two different explanations for this. One is that the man gallantly walks nearest the kerb so as to protect his lady companion from the traffic, or the contents of chamber pots being emptied from upstairs windows. This suggests, though, that promenading couples only ever walk on the left-hand pavement. The other explanation is that the lady is on the left so that she may tuck her trembling little hand into the crook of his arm, leaving his sword (or to give it a contemporary twist, his credit card) hand, free.

These days it doesn't much matter, really – unless your

---

1. The illustrator of this very book, in fact.

2. By the present author.

"You hypocrite! First remove the orange from your own mouth so that you can spit clearly in your brother's (generic) eye"

companion is hard of hearing, in which case you should walk on the hearing-aid side; or they are wearing an embarrassing hat, in which case I'd walk on the other side of the street.

A true lady uses a butter knife in private

This is palpably absurd. A true lady has servants to butter her bread.

Eat what is put before you

This applies to adults, not children. Of children, all that we require is that they refrain from giving the plate a sideways shove of disgust while announcing "I'm not eating *that* muck!" I'm happy to say that my sons have now reached the stage of being polite in their refusal to eat muck.

Adults, on the other hand, can reasonably be expected to tackle anything that is put in front of them. Claiming allergies is an absolute last resort, as it is good manners to alert your host beforehand if you are a coeliac-suffering vegetarian with nut and dairy intolerances. I was a terribly picky eater as a child, but nowadays can cope with most foods apart from offal (memories of school liver with the tubes showing) and even then, I find if I cut it into small enough pieces I can swallow it without chewing.[3]

---

3. If you are trying this technique, check first that someone in the room knows how to do the Heimlich manoeuvre.

CHAPTER 18
Emotional health

E motional health is something we think about quite a lot nowadays. In previous generations worrying about low self-esteem and suppressed anger wasn't on the agenda. You just knuckled down and got on with life. In fact, anger was *meant* to be suppressed. Denial was positively encouraged. You were supposed to count to ten and keep a stiff upper lip. Betraying your feelings was bad form, like letting your slip show. These days we know better, of course.

Anger – how to get in touch with your inner psychopath

Inside every good clergy wife there is a red-eyed wolf woman waiting to escape. The problem is how to let her out for a spot of exercise without innocent parishioners getting their heads ripped off. Personally, I like to go for a good judo training session.[1]

It is not just clergy wives who struggle with how to express anger. Many Christians do. We have not been taught, exactly, that anger is wrong. Jesus was angry now and then, therefore anger can't be sinful in itself. It's just that every expression of it – apart from driving moneylenders out of the temple, perhaps – is sinful. We have a concept of righteous, godly anger, but somehow this is never quite the right description of how we feel when the person in front of us in the "10 items or less" queue at the supermarket has 12 items in their basket.

One helpful route to try is Gestalt therapy, which involves punching a cushion instead of the person who has annoyed you. I actually prefer stamping on polystyrene, but that's just a personal thing.

---

1. There are other sports, but stop and think for a minute – how many of them allow you to throttle people till their eyes pop without being sent off?

Jealousy and how to tackle it

My sisters and I had a little catchphrase we used in connection with anyone successful, wealthy, beautiful and slim. We would look at one another solemnly and say, "Yes, but are they *happy*?" And after a long pause the other one would reply, "Probably."

Envy is an unattractive thing. I'm afflicted by it every time I read one of those home improvement magazines and see people with their converted chapels or Tudor water mills, doing their bedrooms up in swathes of raw ivory silk and finding antique Venetian mirrors for two quid in car boot sales. I'm also vulnerable when I read the book review sections and see younger sexier writers being lionised. This is one of the very few circumstances when having heard good old-fashioned fire-and-brimstone sermons in your childhood stands you in good stead. If you know yourself to be a hell-deserving sinner, anything else comes as a bonus.

A sudden pang of envy can be very instructive, if you bother to track it back to its source. It is generally telling you something interesting. Why does *that* thing make me jealous, not something else? I'm not jealous of people with fast cars or pedigree dogs or luxurious handlebar moustaches, for instance. I've noticed over the years that my hunger to own a converted chapel is always at its most acute when I'm feeling restless in the place where I actually live. I think envy is an emotional displacement activity. I could counsel you in my best Pollyanna style to think cheerful thoughts and count your blessings, but let's face it, it's more fun to open a bottle of champagne.

All reactions are equally valid

What does that mean, *valid*? Legitimate? Acceptable? This is cobblers. All reactions are equally *there*. Some, however, are better than others. Punching someone in the face is *not* as good as walking away.

Remember your Newton: Every action has an equal and opposite reaction. If you *do* punch someone hard in the face, you will probably break your hand. Use a large plank of wood instead.

"Calling me a stupid burk might well be a valid reaction but will add 2 years to the 5 for the emotional displacement activity and 15 for the Newton on Mr Herman in the corner shop."

How to be happy

You are, you are! It's behind you, but if you turn round, it will whisk itself away out of your sight. The pursuit of happiness may be an American constitutional right, but that's a bit like having the title deeds to the rainbow's end.[2] As we have already noted, our Puritan forebears were in the habit of treating each day as though it were their last. I'm sometimes keenly aware that I am only ever a phone call away from tragedy. And when the police officers stand on your doorstep breaking the bad news, who cares then that your partner drops their underwear on the bathroom floor and that you are the only one in the house who puts the bins out?

How to be a miserable git

Many people need no advice here, but for those of you with a relentlessly cheery disposition, here are some pointers:

- shake your head while speaking
- predict failure
- say "Hah!" bitterly
- point out that the rain is rotting the plants
- point out that the good weather is drying out the plants
- relate your medical history whenever possible
- oppose everything
- say "Our old vicar never/always did *x*"
- sum up any diatribe with the words "Still, mustn't grumble"

Remember: the glass is not only half empty, it is chipped and somebody has just knocked it over.

How to be sad

By sad, I mean down at heart, rather than "sad" in the Young Person sense of the word, where the semantic range covers everything that parents do, say or wear. One easy way to become sad is to watch the

---

2. One of my cousins, as a small girl, very astutely enquired *which* end of the rainbow the gold was buried. I think that shows commendable caution.

news or read the papers. It's good to be sad now and then. Lent is the traditional time for this in the Anglican Church. This is not just because we have given up booze. It is a period when we can look afresh at the suffering and death of Christ, and stand mentally before the cross with the weight of the world on our shoulders. Sometimes "when the woes of life o'ertake us" (as the hymn writer puts it) that is the only place we can stand. When I see pictures of war and devastation and famine and all the human suffering that goes along with them, to cut straight to the empty tomb feels too glib. There are times when all you can do is stand helpless before the image of the suffering God. There is no other "answer" capable of bearing the weight.

PART IV

The perfect lifestyle

Introduction

The word "Lifestyle" is an odd one. It is often used in connection with the word "alternative" as a polite euphemism for "homosexual". People with "alternative lifestyles" are *actually* people with alternative sexual habits, aren't they? Not, say, strict Sabbatarians who live in tree-houses and communicate entirely by yodelling.

But have no fear! The following section is *not* on how to be perfectly gay. In fact, if I were gay, I think I'd be pretty fed up by now reading books by straight Christians telling me what was what. No, to be honest with you, I am using "Lifestyle" as a catch-all heading for a whole bunch of chapters that I couldn't think how else to categorise.

CHAPTER 19
How not to be bored

Intelligent people are never bored. That's what my mother always used to say to us. In fact, she's still saying it. She said to my nephew a few months ago, "Well as I always used to tell your mother, *intelligent people are never bored.*" At this my nephew reared up in indignation and said "So *that's* where Mum got it from!"

It is, without a doubt, the most annoying thing you can say to a child complaining of boredom. Except, possibly, "If you're bored, *I'll* find you something to do!" As every child knows, this "something" is "tidy your room" and they instantly conclude that they are not *that* bored. And let's face it, nobody is that bored. There are only two reasons for tidying – shame, and having an urgent tax return to fill in.

What is boredom?

When I was growing up I pronounced any activity I couldn't master in about three seconds as boring. The standard teen definition is "Anything grown-ups want you to do." According to my dictionary, boredom is "a state of being bored", and "to bore" means "to produce a hole by use of a drill, auger or rotary cutting tool". It is possible to be locked in a state of such mind-numbing tedium that the prospect of making holes in yourself with a rotary cutting tool begins to seem attractive. So presumably, if you are totally bored, you may end up being a human colander.

But here's the heart of it: a thing is only boring if you'd rather be doing something else. Childhood boredom is the state of wishing you were doing something else, but not knowing what that might be (other than nothing your mother helpfully suggests).

Children are most in danger of getting bored during school holidays. This is why we pay good money to hire a cottage in the country, which leads neatly on to my first section:

Things to do on rainy holidays

1. Light a fire. (Make sure the cottage has a fireplace.) Children enjoy helping make fires. Once you've got a good blaze going you can toast various things like crumpets, marshmallows, bits of Lego, the paper you hadn't finished reading, cushions and rugs.

2. Go swimming. If your children are over eight, you can let them swim by themselves. This leaves you free to sit by the pool in the echoing din of screams, on an uncomfortable plastic chair, your eyes watering from the chlorine, reading a good book and trying to eat a Snickers bar without your children seeing.

3. Visit a National Trust property. Most of the sense of achievement here is in managing to arrive outside the gates of the property you have selected on a day and at a time when it is open. Some stately homes are only open between May and October, others are shut on Fridays, with the occasional wild card in small print like *Closed Bank Holiday Mondays*. Having established that this is a Wednesday in July, and therefore, as far as it is humanly possible to tell, Blitherthwaite Hall is open to the public, you make a picnic (to avoiding taking out a second mortgage at Blitherthwaite Hall Tea Shop), bundle the children, wellies and coats into the car, and head for your destination. You arrive and find the gates closed. "Not open till 2pm", reads one of your children, helpfully. It is 11.30am. Too long to wait, too far from the cottage to go back and return at 2. "Well, we could do the rhododendron walk," Mum suggests brightly. "That's open!" Then it emerges that you are three wellies short. The thought of hopping with whinging children round a dripping garden is suddenly too much. You eat the picnic in the car, drive back to the cottage, collect the swimming stuff, go swimming, then go home again and light a fire.

Boring people

I have a theory that nobody is inherently boring. They only *seem* boring because of this business of preferring to do something else other than listen to them telling you about their hip operation. The dis-ease we experience – the suppressed yawns, the surreptitious glances at our watch, the restless shifting from foot to foot – is because we are trapped in time. We are frustrated because we'd rather be playing golf, or drilling holes in our leg with a rotary cutting tool. If, however, we had all eternity to play with, we could listen to our companion with ungrudging generosity, knowing that however long they wombled on, we would still get our eighteen holes – whether that be on the golf course or in the upper thigh. I'm not trying to imply that in heaven we will be locked in eternal conversation with the type of people we duck into car parts shops to avoid; just that without the constraint of time, boredom cannot exist.

Coping with boring sermons

I think that it was during long sermons as a child that I first began learning the craft of being a novelist. These days I don't feel quite the same liberty to daydream, on the grounds that if someone has put the effort into preparing a sermon, I should put the effort into listening. This tends to break down when I suspect that the preacher is winging it. If they haven't put the work in, then frankly, why the heck should I? Being angry is a good way of getting through tedious sermons. You will find you are paying attention simply in order to become more indignant at the preacher's theology, or lack of it.

Keeping children quiet in church is a demanding business. Over the years we have had several trusty standbys. Eating the pew sheet has now given way to drawing on it or using it for paper aeroplanes. I have to confess that I have played "drawing consequences" in church with my older son (where the first person draws a hat, folds the page down, the second draws the head, and so on). But since the occasion when we got hysterical during an ordination, we've had to stop. He also used to play "sermon cricket" (scoring the match with the help of umpiring signals from the preacher), but he gave that up, too, after a rather hectoring sermon in which both teams were given out in two minutes flat.

Meetings and Synods

Things you *should not* do during boring meetings/synods

- clean your ears with a paper clip

- pick your nose
- pick someone else's nose
- take all your clothes off and run screaming from the building

Things you *may* do during a boring meeting/synod

- daydream
- doodle
- pass round a bag of Liquorice All Sorts
- write the first line of a limerick and pass it on

CHAPTER 20
Hobbies

The word "hobby" is problematical. It tends to diminish the activity concerned. "Oh, it's just his little hobby," a wife might say disparagingly of her husband's lifelong collection of rare first editions. Obsessions always look ludicrous from the outside. This is particularly true in England, where it is against the law to be passionate about anything, except possibly football during the World Cup.[1] The difficulty is knowing what else to call a hobby. A *pastime*? That makes it sound as though you only undertake this activity in order to while away the hours. A *leisure activity*? Again, the phrase is belittling, making it sound like something you do to relax, something lightweight to set against the real business of work. Anyone in the grip of an obsession knows it's nothing like that. The word "passion" probably comes closest, but to say "my passion is for collecting matchboxes" is to lay yourself open to ridicule. We will have to stick with hobby, despite its limitations.

How to find the perfect hobby

The perfect hobby is one which you find thoroughly absorbing, yet which doesn't bore the pants off everyone else. Ideally, it keeps you out from under other people's feet for hours at a time when they are busy. Or, to put it another way, it enables you to slope off for hours at a time when other people are busy and there is a risk they may co-opt your services. Reading a book may be a splendid hobby, but you will find that if you sit reading while other people are flying about the place tidying up before the in-laws arrive, you will get your head bitten off.

---

1. I was particularly struck by this while I was living in New Zealand. The informal national motto there seems to be "Have a Go!" As a Curate I Know pointed out, the English equivalent is "I'd be crap at that."

Hobbies may helpfully be divided into various categories: physical, spiritual and mental. For example: football is a *physical* hobby, taking a retreat to a monastery *spiritual*, trainspotting, *mental*.[2]

The perfect physical hobby

There are *three* aspects to physical hobbies. They get you *fit*. They stop you getting *fat*. They are *fun*. (Just proving I am a real Evangelical, after all.) They can also cost a *fortune*, but as far as I know, I am only ever allowed to find *three* significant things to say on any subject, so we'll have to gloss over the expense involved in physical hobbies.

There are many different physical hobbies, to be sure. They can, broadly speaking, be divided into team sports and solo efforts. At the risk of making sweeping gender generalisations, men tend towards the former (5-a-side football, cricket) while women are more drawn to individual events (step aerobics, going to the gym). Squash, a popular male hobby (until their knees give out and they have to take up mountain biking), *appears* to be a solo sport, but in fact, it involves having a partner to play against, so I am treating it as a team sport.

This division (and I know there are exceptions, like squash-playing women) comes about because men tend to emphasise the *fun* aspect of sport. It's a chance to be with your mates, shout blokish abuse at one another and hive off to the pub afterwards. Women emphasise the not getting *fat* aspect. A woman's exercise class may well be a joyless experience, but she will carry on grimly, regardless. For several weeks on the trot! Especially after Christmas, or when she is haunted by the imminent prospect of herself on a beach hanging lardily over her bikini bottoms.

I can only speak from my own experience. Exercise classes I find tedious and frequently humiliating. I sometimes go running, but running isn't a hobby, really, is it? It's more of a grim duty. And for the better-endowed woman, there is also the drollness of passing males to be endured, some of whom helpfully shout out jocular terms for breasts. Oh is *that* what they are! And there was me thinking I was running along with a couple of carriage clocks strapped to my chest! You know something? One of the worst things about being a vicar's

---

2. In the sense that you have to be mental to do it.

wife is never being able to stick two fingers up, in case the offenders turn up in church one day.

So, no, running is not what I term a hobby. I know you see these so-called "Fun Runs" advertised, but are they *really* fun? I have images of myself trying and failing to slip-stream old ladies up hills, and that's never good for the self-esteem. Sprinting is fun, but only if you win.

There is only one hobby for me: judo. "Judo" means "the gentle way". That's the famous Japanese sense of humour. People are often surprised when I tell them I do judo, but we clergy wives don't get all that many opportunities to roll around the floor with a dozen sweaty blokes, so we have to take our fun where we can.

I started judo when my two sons suddenly clamoured to be allowed to learn some martial art involving kidney chops, blood-curdling cries and cool Bruce Lee style headbands. I couldn't find any karate classes at a suitable hour of the day, so I ended up taking them along to a judo session I'd seen advertised. I walked in to the hall where people were putting mats out and said to the coach, "Two new ones for you." He looked me in the eye and asked "Are you coming on the mat as well?" And a sudden and wholly unexpected "YES PLEASE!" welled up inside me. I'd done judo for about a year as a girl, and hadn't had a really good scrap since. It was time to get back in touch with my inner tomboy.

There is some confusion about the purpose of judo amongst those who know little about martial arts. "I suppose it's a good way of keeping fit," people say to me in a perplexed way. To which I reply, "True, but I'm there for the fighting." There is no better stress-buster known to humankind than giving someone a jolly good scragging. (Think how church AGM's could be improved if we introduced some form of wrestling into the decision-making process!) I think rugby occupies a similar niche, but it's outdoors and cold and muddy, so yuck to rugby. Incidentally, my sons both gave up judo after a year, one of them complaining it was "too violent". Perhaps those judging by appearances might think he's right, all the bruises and black eyes and so on, but I think that's a rather glib and superficial conclusion to draw. (See above Chapter 7, on how to lift blood stains from white clothes.) The other splendid thing about judo is the baggy white pyjamas. A deeply egalitarian outfit. Everyone's bum looks big in them.

The perfect spiritual hobby

The first thing you need to sort out here is whether you are essentially an extrovert or an introvert. This will determine whether you will need convivial company to refresh you, or hermit-like isolation. For instance, an introvert may relish the idea of a 14-day silent Ignatian retreat, while your extrovert will seek out some huge bless-up in a holiday camp, involving lots of long worship sessions and the constant interrupting of the speaker by clapping every other sentence.

Many ministers and clergy are introverts who are obliged, by the public nature of their duties, to adopt extrovert roles. This means that they require long periods by themselves to recharge their batteries. So when you next see your pastor shouldering his or her golf bag and heading for some lonely course in the middle of the week, don't think, "Oh *I* see! Hard at work as usual! Wish *I* only worked one day a week!" etc. The poor souls are doing what repair work they can.[3]

The Perfect Mental Hobby

There really is only one, isn't there? Reading. Of course, you *may* play chess or Scrabble, if you wish, but in my experience these tend to shade over into the physical when tempers flare and punches are thrown. By reading I don't mean worthy Christian paperbacks about how God has miraculously worked in other people's lives, and would in yours, too, surely, if only you weren't too sinful and rebellious to claim the victory. Handbooks of this kind – on how to organise God into moving in our time and get him answering prayer properly – are all very well in their place, that place being the bin. No, I'm talking about real hard-nosed secular books in all their muck and brilliance. Don't be afraid of them. If you are worried that they will undermine your faith, then you might like to take a closer look at what you are building on. Of course, *good* Christian paperbacks are a different proposition. Ooh, yes, you should definitely read *those*.

---

3. In the case of clergy, golf counts as a spiritual activity. They have enough of religion the rest of the time.

Ten perfect things to do in an odd moment

- listen to some Palestrina
- bake a cake
- go for a walk in the dark and look through people's windows
- write someone a letter
- plant something
- open a bottle of champagne
- sit on the top of a bus and go somewhere new
- look through your old photos
- have a long bath
- start the second layer of chocolates before the first is finished

"It might seem like a perfect night to you but the rest of society thinks it odd to take photos of people in the bath through their windows."

CHAPTER 21
Perfect meals

The perfect dinner party

If you aren't middle class, look away now. Dinner parties are the province of the middle classes – in England, at any rate. If you are very posh, you probably say "supper" (or "sups" even). This can cause all manner of inter-class confusion when invitations are issued – people turning up at the wrong time expecting the wrong meal.

When I was growing up we had "breakfast", "dinner" and "tea", with the possibility of "supper" last thing at night. Even now, when calling my children to their evening meal, I shout "Tea time, boys!" Well, actually, I usually shout "Lunch!" then, realising that's not right, I randomly shout other meals until I hit upon the correct one, so it comes out like this: "Boys! Br-lu-din-tea time!" And then I swiftly add "No, you can't!" in answer to the question, Can we eat it in front of the TV. Followed by, "I don't care if it *is* the Simpsons!"

That's what happens if it's just us. If we are having people round for an evening meal, it becomes "dinner"; although we never actually say that. We say "You must come round for a meal sometime. What about next Friday, at 8?" We trust to convention that they will understand, and not turn up at 8am expecting breakfast.

My fantasy dinner party

Sometimes I feel so brim full of Christian charity and niceness in my role as vicar's wife that I give way to evil thoughts. Please pray for me. One of my secret ambitions is to host the dinner party from hell. First of all you invite people you know won't get on: staunch feminists and devout Anglo-Catholics, retired army majors and Labour councillors; all those prickly difficult people you know, along with those famed for their lack of tact. For good measure add someone who has recently undergone major surgery and enjoys talking about it. If you also know someone incredibly squeamish, so much the better. Any work put into the seating plan will be well rewarded.

The next step is to serve embarrassing food. Your menu might include:

- sea food still in its shell
- ambiguous garnishes e.g. entire baby octopus/dandelion flowers/chicken feet
- entire animals – e.g. lobster, guinea fowl – presented in a lifelike way
- offal
- apparent foreign bodies e.g. blackened whole almonds[1]
- long spaghetti with sloppy sauce
- rock hard meringue nests which explode/fly across table

The experience can be heightened by:

- inexplicable cutlery/tools
- chopsticks
- dispensing with a table*

*especially if the plates are shallow and the sauce runny

Don't forget: pink food dye will make chicken look dangerously undercooked.

Enjoy!

The perfect breakfast

The perfect breakfast is served in a Paris hotel, when some grumbling Parisian lumbers up to your cheap room in the attic, boots the bottom of your door and bellows, "*Le petit déjeuner*, you steupide Eenglishe types!" (the last bit being muttered inaudibly). Ignore the ill humour radiating from the disgruntled domestic, for the meal will be delicious. The bread rolls and croissants will have come straight from the local

---

1. These uncannily resemble cockroaches

bakery, having been made that very morning. The coffee will be all that coffee in a Parisian hotel should be. Wait a few moments to allow the waddling shape to make its way back, all the way back, down to the basement, then call room service and ask for milk. If you already have milk, ask for hot water. Use your imagination. As you recline, showering croissant crumbs on the hotel sheets, contemplate the galleries you will visit, the boulevards you will stroll down, the expensive perfumeries you will linger wistfully outside until your partner is worn down and buys you what you want. As they say in France, *Parfait*!

The perfect brunch

You will probably have to go to America to find this. Make sure you select a place serving buffet style eat-all-you-can brunch. The idea is to load yourself up with enough fat and carbohydrate to see a family of twelve through a particularly hard winter, then go back for seconds. You will encounter new culinary delights. There will be hash browns and grits, and other things that look and sound like the kind of thing your Granny served to her chickens from a pail. Don't be deterred. It is here that you will learn the difference between muffins and *English* muffins, the latter presumably being the kind purchased from the muffin man who lives on Drury Lane; rather than the blueberry or chocolate chip monsters which would pass for birthday cakes in the UK. Make sure you experiment with new combinations of food while you're at it. Maple syrup on bacon is a firm American favourite; but there is no reason you shouldn't put ketchup on your pop tarts if you feel like it. This is, after all, the country that gave us jello salads.

The perfect elevenses

I'm rather afraid that the grand English institution of elevenses is dying out. When I was a girl it usually meant a beaker of (weak) squash and a rich-tea biscuit, about which, what can we say, other than what my father always said: "If that's *rich* tea, then I dread to think what poor tea is like." On a good day it would be ginger nuts (the perfect dunking biscuit) and milk. If I was staying with my Grandma I used to get a glass of Lucozade and a piece of what she called "praline bar", which was a chocolate biscuit cake with glacé cherries and fruit in, and a nice thick layer of Cake Brand milk chocolate on top. Occasionally I might get a homemade cream horn or brandy snap instead. (She was in many ways the perfect Grandma.)

Elevenses is giving way to a quick mid-morning coffee. Eating at this time of day is increasingly seen as a sign of weakness. This is depressing.

The perfect morning tea

There is, however, one far-flung corner of the globe where the tradition of elevenses is alive and well. I'm speaking of New Zealand. The only difference is that they call it "morning tea". It is here that home-baking skills flourish and are displayed. Woe unto that housewife, even if she be a busy career woman, who serves up *shop cake*.

The perfect lunch

The perfect lunch is one you are taken out to by someone else who is paying.

The perfect dinner

Ditto.

The perfect supper

This is usually *either* a bowl of cereal, *or* toast (always cook double what you expect to eat, because everyone else will suddenly want a slice once they smell it, even if you have just asked them and they have said no) *or* anything you bolt while standing in front of an open fridge, e.g. cold sausage, leftover trifle, etc.

CHAPTER 22
Parties

There are many occasions for throwing parties in this poor fallen world. They brighten our days and function as reminders of that great messianic banquet spoken of in the Scriptures – though some are better reminders than others, of course. In fact, parties for young children can remind one of hell. So let's tackle that subject first.

The perfect children's party

Tinies

When children are tiny the party is little more than an opportunity for the weary Mums (or possibly Dads) to slump in someone's sitting room and drink coffee and eat cake, while the children crawl around grabbing one another's hair and plastic toys and spilling hot coffee on themselves and being rushed off to Casualty.

There will be presents, of course, because nobody is quite callous enough simply to give the child what it most likes at this age: the packaging and wrapping paper. There will be a homemade chocolate cake that hasn't quite worked, covered with chocolate icing and perhaps studded with Smarties, with one candle leaning drunkenly in the centre. The children will be given rice cakes or plain biscuits because nobody wants to face the mess that a one-year-old makes with a chunk of chocolate cake. The mothers will eat the cake, which, although it hasn't quite worked, is still undeniably chocolate, and as such acceptable. They aren't worried about their weight, because once they stop breast feeding, the extra pounds will just drop off, tra la! Everyone knows that. And anyway, they'll start exercising and dieting and things. But there's not much point now, especially if they are planning several more kids, so go on then, just a small bit.

4s–8s

When children get bigger the party needs a bit more organising. The most important thing is to make sure you've got a good adult-to-child ratio. This is best achieved by enticing adults along with the promise of wine. Let the children run amok. This is what they want at this stage. They don't want to be made to play games. (If they insist, try "Dead Lions".)

If it is summer, let them run around the garden. Call it a "Pirate Party" and let them play in the paddling pool and water pistol one another. (Dads, remember to reserve the Pump-action Super Soaker with 12 gallon tank for yourself.) Whatever else you do, DON'T FORGET THE PARTY BAGS! These must be filled with noxious brightly coloured sweets with a half-life of 2000 years, a balloon, a selection of useless plastic toys and a piece of damp cake wrapped in a party napkin and looking as if it's been sat on.

9s–11s

The older child despises parties. Parties are for *babies*. He or she would rather take a few friends for a hugely expensive treat to Legoland. They can generally be fobbed off with a cinema or water park trip. Girls can be persuaded to have what they obscurely call a "sleepover", but which parents know as a "wakeover", and a chance to experiment with nail varnish and temporary tattoos.

At the younger end of this age group there is an alternative route to go down. You can organise a party that *nobody else in the class has had*. Novelty = kudos, if your children have the confidence to carry it off. We had a Native American party for our younger son a while back, hiring Red Horse and his squaw, who came and set up their totem poles in our sitting room and entertained the children with stories and songs and dances. At the height of one of these blood-curdling pagan war dances the phone rang. It was the Bishop, wanting to talk to a VIK. "I'll just get him," I shouted over the wild yipping and ululations and drumming. Perhaps I should have called, with my hand half-over the mouthpiece, "And turn down the volume on the Saturday afternoon Western you are watching there in the sitting room!"

The teens

I'm afraid that if you want your children to appreciate their party, then there is no alternative to letting them do what they want, and uncomplainingly footing the bill. The more opposition you put up, the bigger the bill is likely to be. Admittedly, all this is still ahead of me as my children aren't teenagers yet. They practise occasionally. My older son likes to lean against things with his arms crossed in a cool way. He also ventures the opinion from time to time that something is *so not fair*. But I am aware that the real storms still lie in the future.

One strategy that I use now, and hope will still work in a few years time, is to ask, "Well, what do you think is reasonable?" The subject in question is usually how many biscuits he can have. The interesting thing is that he generally – after optimistically suggesting 27 billion – names a figure smaller than the one I would have been prepared to settle for. After a show of reluctance, I consent.

I think this could transfer to teenage party planning. When your teenager asks belligerently how many they can invite, ready to shout "Only *x*??!! That is SO NOT FAIR!!", you take the wind out of their sails by inquiring mildly "Well, what do you think is reasonable?" – as if talking adult to adult. The chances are they will want fewer than you think.[1]

The perfect adult party

The world is divided into people who think Hooray! and those who groan Oh no! when they are invited to a fancy dress party. I am an enthusiastic member of the former group. I confess to having little patience with those who can't organise themselves into some kind of a costume. It's not *that* hard, for heaven's sake! My enthusiasm is probably a direct result of my Mum being good at this kind of thing. My sisters and I used to win first prize every year at the village fete. YESS!! Not that winning prizes is important for the Christian. One time we went as a six-legged dragon led along by the little princess, our youngest sister. I was the middle pair of legs, which sums up all that is wrong with being a middle child. You don't get to gnash the

---

1. I expect I shall read this in five years' time and laugh hollowly at this section on How to be Perfectly Self-Deluding.

cardboard jaws, you don't get to wag the tail. You're the bit in the middle nobody looks at.[2]

For a fancy dress party to go with a swing, you do need a theme. This helps focus people's creativity, and means you can make simple costume suggestions to the whingers.

Good themes

- 1920s
- Hollywood
- Red, White and Blue
- The Good, the Bad and the Ugly
- Heroes and Villains

Bad themes

- Tarts and Vicars (a bit of a busman's holiday, frankly)
- Great Evangelists of the 1970s

---

2. This can turn a middle child into a bit of a show off, incidentally; so if you have a middle child, go easy on them, or they might grow up into writers, and say horrible things about you in books, like You Never Let Me Wear Platforms, Mother, You Ruined My Life.

CHAPTER 23
The perfect place

The perfect place is, almost invariably, *somewhere else*. This is because the hardest place to be content is where you are. The golden age, the good times, that heaven-on-earth, all tend to move around in a tricksy way, receding before us, then suddenly popping up behind us, so that we are forever glimpsing them in our rear view mirror as we are leaving. It only requires our restless presence in a place for it to acquire imperfections.

Listen, that perfect tropical island paradise has mosquitoes, my good friends. Trust me, I've been there. It also has sand and intolerable humidity and rain and ants and cocks crowing outside your window at 4am and no Earl Grey teabags. Worst of all, it has the nagging sense that you are selfishly using up a space in tropical paradise that could be better used by someone else. Why, why can't I enjoy it? you berate yourself. Why, why, can't we enjoy living in the affluent West, where we know we won't starve or get carted off to prison or see our loved ones shot without trial? Why are we wasting our lives wishing we were a stone lighter and on holiday, or that we could afford to get the kitchen done?

How to find the perfect place

How incredibly hard it is to lie still under the microscope of the present moment, and not sink back into the comfort of the past, or skedaddle into some vividly imagined future. This is me, now, in this place, at this moment, and all I will ever have is a sequence of such moments to inhabit. This is as good or as bad as it gets. Which means that if you are looking for the perfect place, the salutary truth is: *you might be in it already.* The odd thing is that people seem to be capable of being content in awful circumstances and miserable in idyllic ones.

Plato and the perfect tea shop

The fact that we can't achieve perfection or find perfect happiness doesn't stop us envisaging such a thing. I, for instance, have a clear idea of what the perfect tea shop is like; that pure platonic form of tea shop from which all earthly tea shops take their tea shopness. I go in quest of this perfect tea shop, though I know that I will not find it in this life.

Perfect places to live

San Francisco is a perfect city to live in. At a distance you might wonder, Why on earth would anyone build a city on a fault line? But when you arrive for the very first time and see it, locked in some permanent magical moody spring, with the bridges, the harbour, Chinatown, the streetcars, all the pastel-coloured houses clinging to the precipitous hills, and – suddenly you say to yourself, Oh, I *see* now.

Wellington in New Zealand is another perfect place to live. It has stunning views across the harbour, where one might write a book such as this, glancing up to watch the inter-island ferries come and go, and the little white yachts leaning on the wind and the occasional pods of killer whales playing in the water. It has the feel of a big cosmopolitan city, but doesn't have the grime and crime. It has more places to buy a decent cappuccino than anywhere else – except possibly heaven, where you won't have to buy them, I hope.

And **Paris**, of course, you don't need me to explain why; and **Bruges** for its perfect little streets and canals and chocolate; and the wild **Northumbrian coast**; and **Mid Wales**; and **Mull**; and **Durham**, City of God; the depths of **Normandy** in August, swooning with hay and cider smells and the night sky raining stars, and not forgetting...

Walsall in the West Midlands, perhaps *the* perfect place to live. It has shops, it has fine civic buildings, an art gallery with panoramic views across the Black Country. It has an arboretum with mature trees and two lakes where you may see crested grebes and kingfishers and feed the baby ducks on the way to school. In the autumn you can enjoy the world famous Walsall Illuminations. It has matey locals, and if you listen hard, you may well be able to understand what they are saying, even if, like me, you are an incomer. Its people are from a multitude of different ethnic backgrounds, which means that no matter what time of year, someone will always be setting off fireworks to celebrate something. It is also near **Birmingham**, which is the perfect city, because it has got just about everything and is much closer than London.[1]

A formula for locating your nearest perfect place:

X [insert name of place you live in] is a perfect place, *because* [list reasons]

A perfect place is:

Somewhere you have

- lived in
- loved

Perfect mini places

It is a human instinct to attempt to create a perfect micro environment. Many people seek to do this with their house. Sometimes married couples discover they have conflicting ideas about what the perfect home looks like. When this happens, the husband may retire from the battlefield and establish an alternative base in the garage, or failing that, in a garden shed or down at the allotments. If he is lucky he may manage to keep a toehold in hostile territory in the form of a study or "den", but there he will be permanently at risk of attack from incoming enemy cushions and IKEA rugs.

Small children also like to make micro environments. These are generally erected in any inconvenient place – on the stairs, in

---

1. It is an interesting geographical fact that Birmingham is no further away from London than London is from Birmingham. Even with the help of maps it is difficult to convince Londoners of this.

doorways, in the loo – and are little fantasy worlds for Lego men and Barbie to live out their complex lives. Seeing this, adults often go to great lengths to buy or construct "play houses" for their offspring. If these are outdoor, permanent structures, the children will not play in them because of the spiders. If they are small, portable houses, such as pop-up tents, they will be dragged by the child to any inconvenient place – e.g. stairs, doorways, loo.

Childhood dens: important information

children *will* play in

- large cardboard box from new kitchen appliance
- large cloth hanging over table
- tent on lawn

children will play *once* in

- expensive wooden Swiss chalet-style playhouse with little window boxes
- expensively constructed tree house

children *won't* play in

- any den of any description within 10m radius of spot where any spider has ever been sighted in the history of the world

CHAPTER 24
Holidays

Types of holiday

There are so many different approaches to the idea of holiday. Broadly speaking, they can be taken *at home* or *away from home*. If they are to be taken away from home, they can be taken *in your home country*, or *abroad*. If you are an astronaut, they could be taken in space, I suppose, but this is what we call *a busman's holiday*.

The origins of "holiday"

In the olden days holidays were "holy days", the days of major festivals, Easter, Christmas, various saints' days, the Feast of the Blessed Translation of Ithamar's Sacred Relics to Holy Rochester – any excuse, really. These occasions usually involved a slap-up meal, a trip to church and various boisterous pagan rites which the church had failed to stamp out properly. People didn't "go away on holiday". If you did that, who would look after the land? The fox would get in the chickens, the cows would get in the corn. Or worse, the Scots would invade.

The only options, if you wanted to get away from it all, were to go off on pilgrimage to some important religious shrine or other; or on a Crusade, forcibly baptising pagans or simply killing them if they didn't see the glorious Gospel light in time.[1]

If we canter on through a few centuries we come upon the phenomenon of the "Grand Tour", which was undertaken by the rich

---

1. Personally, I think the unchurched should bear this in mind when they turn up wanting their babies "done" and are narked to discover the vicar wants them to sit through some kind of basic Christianity course first. At least the vicar isn't holding a sword to their throat when he or she asks them if they "turn to Christ". A small point, but an important one.

"Are we nearly there yet?"

as a means of acquiring a bit of cosmopolitan gloss. The poor were far too busy on the land or down the mines or in the mills to go in for any of that namby-pamby travelling abroad nonsense. Leisure was for toffs and big girls' blouses. Eventually, the poor relented and drew back somewhat from their hard-line stance and agreed to go off to Blackpool – but only once a year, mind. Then it was straight back to work, no messing.

I hope you don't feel sorry for the poor, here. That would be a mistake. If you knew the poor you'd realise they actually *enjoy* working their guts out for a pittance; the way everyone who hunts knows foxes actually *enjoy* being hunted.

These days, as we know, holidays are enshrined in law. They are compulsory. You *have* to go on holiday. If you are English and between the ages of 18–30 you *must* spend 90% of your time drunk. You *may also* break up bars, throw bottles, get laid, punch people and get thrown in jail by locals who fail to understand that damage to persons/property is just the English way of having a good time. Above all – *you must enjoy it*. Not to enjoy a holiday which has absorbed so much money and in which you have invested so much hope – that would be a crime indeed!

The perfect holiday

To find your perfect holiday, you need to sort yourself into various categories. Before you book a holiday ask:

1. Am I the type who likes to
   a. go somewhere new?
   b. return to somewhere I have previously enjoyed?

2. Do I like to holiday
   a. alone/just my family?
   b. with others/other families?

3. Am I
   a. comfort loving?
   b. stupid?

4. Do I like
   a. beaches?
   b. mountains/lakes?
   c. theme parks?*

5. Do I prefer to
   a. travel about?
   b. stay put?

By answering these simple questions and *communicating the answers* to the others you will be travelling with, you will save yourselves a lot of misery.

*If you answered **c** to this question you must be under 18, and therefore you have no say, so stop reading this quiz immediately. Once you start *paying* for your holidays you start having a choice, OK? No representation without taxation, I say.

Holidaying at home

You will notice that I didn't call this section "the perfect holiday at home". This is because spending a holiday at home is never perfect, is it? Even if it gives you that perfect opportunity to do the kitchen. It is especially not perfect for anyone who works from home all the rest of the time. Sometimes, however, there is nothing else (or more bluntly, no money) for it. You cannot go away.

Here are some hints on how to make that time at home into a holiday:

- open a bottle of champagne[2]
- unplug the phone
- shift the furniture round
- paint your downstairs loo a mad colour
- get in takeaways
- read

---

2. It is my practice throughout this book to use the word "champagne" as a synonym for "cheap cava".

If you have small children you might like to try some of the following educational and fun activities:

- turn the sitting room into a pirate's ship/smugglers' den
- bake cookies
- sing jolly songs
- go to the library
- make salt dough
- go swimming
- make more cookies
- stick children in front of TV
- shout at children
- burst into tears
- feel like abject failure
- ring Grandma and see if she'll have them
- open bottle of champagne

What is a holiday for?

Sadly, for many of us a holiday is an opportunity to fall out with our nearest and dearest and come down with flu. This is because the act of going on holiday releases the tension which has been holding everything together. Look out for those danger signs ahead of time. If you hear yourself thinking, "I'll just keep going till we're on holiday, it's only *x* weeks/days", then watch out. The way to have a perfect holiday is by not overworking the rest of the time, otherwise you will find your inner PA has pencilled in a migraine for the first two days.

When our children were tiny a VIK worked out that we both saw holidays as the time when we had the right to have a break. Unless I got time off from childcare, a holiday was actually worse than being at home – all the same slog but without the support networks and routines that made it possible to get to the end of the day with both children still alive. From his point of view, a VIK had been slaving away over a hot church all quarter and wanted time to slump without small people swarming over him and being sick on the thriller he was trying to read. Once we'd worked out we were both feeling aggrieved, we were able to cut some kind of deal and things improved.

CHAPTER 25
Perfect transport

What does the Bible have to say about modes of transportation? Well, firstly there are animal modes – camel, ass, horse, mule, colt, etc. Then there is the war chariot, as demonstrated by Jehu, who drove "very furiously".[1] I know people who like to believe that the roar of David's triumph is an early reference to motorbikes, but I think we all know that this is wishful thinking.

The dangers of creeping liberalism

As we are all aware, it is fatal to contextualise and reduce the timeless truths of Scripture to a set of rules which merely apply to a particular day and age. Motor vehicles were unknown in biblical times. Therefore, Christians should not drive cars. Because if you give way on this particular point, where will it all end? Cars are the slippery slope, and so-called believers who drive them are kidding themselves. As Evangelicals we need to be especially on our guard here. If we lightly set aside the Bible on the issue of the internal combustion engine, we will find ourselves dispensing with its teaching on the atoning death of Christ. If a donkey was good enough for the Lord Jesus, it should be good enough for us. Guard the precious deposit, my friends!

The perfect car

For those of you too hopelessly compromised by woolly liberalism to see the truth in what I have just said, here's some common sense instead. The perfect car is one that reliably gets you from A to B. This is when A is sufficiently distant from B to mean you can't easily walk it, i.e., more than a mile, you lazy lumps. This is all that a car needs to

---

1. See above, "Bloke Driving", Chapter 16.

"*The churchwardens would be grateful if <u>that</u> deposit could be placed on the roses by the east door!*"

do. Having said that, the other day I saw a woman in her 70s driving a natty open-topped red sports car. She was wearing a red head scarf which exactly matched the car. I thought the whole effect was rather dashing.[2] This is by way of saying cars can also be fun, if that's your bag. Personally, I think the fun went out of it all along with runner boards and picnic hampers strapped on the back. All I want is a car that won't break down on me one dark rainy night in the middle of nowhere. Although power-assisted steering is handy, come to think of it. Manoeuvring a car without it is like wrestling a moose.

Public transport

I omitted the word "perfect" from that heading as I didn't want to provoke snorts of outright derision. But we can all picture what a perfect public transport system might look like, can't we? If we've been to Switzerland. Cheap and reliable, would be two key concepts here. If we had cheap and reliable public transport, we'd all leave our cars at home. Wouldn't we? Given the state of the climate, I can't escape the conclusion we have a duty to walk or catch a bus or train whenever we can. The freedom to drive our own car whenever and wherever we want is not an inalienable human right, any more than being happy or successful are. They are not "standard" as they say in the car trade.

I actually like buses and trains. They offer me a better chance to think and gaze and read (and throw up, if I attempt the latter on a bus). I dare say if I had to commute long distances on a daily basis, the charm would wear off, especially if my train were routinely late or cancelled.

The perfect response to commuter hell

This can be summed up in a single word: ESCAPE. There are, as ever in the Evangelical world, *three ways* in which you can do this.

Spiritual Escape. If you are trapped in a cramped train or stranded on a wet cold platform, you can see this time as a gift. You might like to

---

2. Unfortunately, two days later she drove it into a bollard and bashed the front in. Fortunately, the bollard prevented her from crashing down a precipitous 100 foot ravine. Extract the moral of your choice from this tale.

catch up on your personal Quiet Time by reading your Bible, or praying God's blessing on those around you. However, if you are already in a vile mood, this suggestion will only make you feel worse by piling the guilt on.

Mental Escape. The old standby of a good book must never be overlooked here. Books are better than broadsheet newspapers in crowded trains, although the latter provide an excellent opportunity for accidentally biffing the person next to you in the face under the guise of sorting the pages out. Make sure you hold your reading material so that your neighbours can't read it over your shoulder. They should jolly well bring their own. Alternatively, this is a good time to rummage around in your treasure box of favourite memories, or use your imagination to create an exciting future. Many people like to listen to music on public transport. This appears to serve a dual purpose – entertaining the person with the headphones and annoying everyone else. For maximum annoyance choose music which consists entirely of the sound "tsh". Mobile phones can be used to similar effect. Remember to keep your voice loud and include the phrase "I'm on the train". On a more charitable note, you might think of intriguing the rest of the compartment by such phrases as *"Me? Apologise to Tony Blair? I think not!"*, or *"I've told you, if Jennifer Lopez is in it, I'm not doing it."*

Physical Escape. Every so often mental and spiritual escapes are not enough and you have to plunge screaming through the crowds in the underground station clawing at your top button as you struggle back up to the light. If you find this happening, pause and ask yourself, *Is my body language trying to tell me something here?* The answer might be small, e.g. *Take a day off*; or it might be large e.g. *Relocate to Devon.* Whatever, take these messages seriously.

The perfect bicycle

The perfect bike, in my opinion, is one ridden by some other fool. I applaud them, but it's not for me. I rode an old sit-up-and-beg bike with a wicker basket on the front round Cambridge for three years, and I feel I've done my time. The chain used to fall off or eat my trouser leg. The tyres got punctures, and the teaspoons pinged dangerously round the kitchen as I tried to mend the holes. Oh, all right, while a VIK[3] tried. The other problem with bikes is the weather. Cycling along the Backs on a glorious May morning is one thing, but a Cambridge winter has to be cycled through to be believed. Whichever direction you are headed, the wind is in your face, and that wind has come straight from Russia.

If you are going to cycle, *wear a helmet*. Feeling a bit of a twit is not a good enough reason to go bare-headed. As an anaesthetist I know once told me in the cheerful tones these medics often adopt: "If you want to end up with massive head injuries on a life support machine, cycling without a helmet is the best way to go about it. It's even better than riding a motor bike."

---

3. He would like to point out that he was only an ordinand at the time, and ought therefore to be described as an OIK.

CHAPTER 26
Perfect music

We are now straying into the minefield of personal taste. There are no rights and wrongs when it comes to music, whether that be in church or out of it.

Yeah, right, as the young people say.

Basically, anyone who prefers modern worship songs to Bach is seriously misled. I say this in a spirit of Christian charity, not snobbery. I feel it only fair to warn you that if you are expecting slushy "Jesus, you are my boyfriend" type stuff in heaven, you are in for a big surprise. Get acclimatised and start listening to the St Matthew Passion now. Just a bit of friendly advice.

Church music

Hymns

These are what we always used to sing in church. I sang them as a child, I sing them now. Hymns are my friends. They comfort me when I am miserable and down at heart. They have become part of the fabric of my soul. They are the bread and meat of my spiritual life. Great doctrinal truths and portions of Scripture are enshrined in them. Modern songs are apt to be like trashy carbohydrates. You can eat a whole packet in one go. Nice at the time, but half an hour later you're hungry again.

The word "hymn" is now often prefaced with "good old traditional", which is a bit patronising in my view, as some of these hymns have been around for centuries and will still be around long after time, like an ever-rolling stream[1], has borne most of the modern stuff away.

Some modern songs will gradually acquire hymn status, of

---

1. As the good old traditional hymn puts it.

course. You can't always tell at the time which will survive the winnowing process. There are some which retain a kind of potent nostalgic charm. Ah, yes! we sigh. Greenbelt 1978! That's when we first sang "How lovely on the mountains"! And all those Vineyard songs still tugging on the heart-strings and conjuring up the fervour of the mid 80s Signs and Wonders era, in much the same way as certain pop songs bring back your O-level year or first disco. I'm not saying this is a bad thing; you just can't expect later generations to feel the same way. As they say, You had to be there.

Worship songs

I don't want to give the impression that I automatically dismiss all modern worship songs out of hand. Unless they contain the words "just" or "really", that is; or are too pornographic in their accidental double entendres.[2] I'm rather fond of several of the Celtic-sounding ones that are popular at the moment, but possibly more because I am a sucker for Scottish ballads, than for any theological content of the lyrics. My older son has recently learnt that I can always be made to weep by a rendition of "Will ye go, lassie, go?" I expect it's my heritage. My paternal grandmother was a Scot. This means I am 25% entitled to make those racist anti-Scots remarks and taunting references to Culloden that occasionally mar my writing.[3]

Plainsong

If you have never heard monks singing Compline in a quiet chapel at the end of a weary day, you have never lived. There is no better way to bind up the broken soul.

Secular music

Opera

Now this will either hearten or dismay you – I haven't yet learnt to love opera. I am saving it for when I retire, when I will also read *War and Peace*, learn Latin and do the dusting.

---

2. Send a plain brown s.a.e. if you want to see a list.

3. I suppose I am also allowed to wear a quarter of a kilt, but the image that conjures up is too disconcerting to contemplate.

Pop music

I get the impression they don't call it "pop music" any more. There are a great many complex sub-divisions which make you want to peer over your half-moon glasses like a High Court judge and enquire "And what *is* this 'Hip-hop' to which you refer?" Teen music comes in various forms, but it has one main function: to shock and antagonise adults. A great deal of the stuff youngsters are into at the moment is racist, sexist, homophobic and violent. If your children listen to this kind of thing, my advice is *take no notice*. They already know you think racism and violence are unacceptable, and they know you are right. If you challenge them you will only force them to justify it as a point of honour. Confine yourself to a look of pained perplexity, as if they were committing an error of taste. You can always play the "this is my house and you abide by my rules" card. You don't have to have it playing where you can hear it. The spirited teen will then go to his or her room and turn the volume right up. Again, ignore it. Then, the next morning at the ungodly hour of, say, 8.30 or 9am, slap on a CD of your own in the room below their bedroom and play *that* at full volume. Perry Como would be a good choice. Or worship songs of the 70s.

Jazz

Is there an intelligent person alive who doesn't enjoy traditional jazz? The modern stuff can be a bit more rarified and is something of an acquired taste, but the sound of a jazz band playing "Ain't Misbehavin'" cheers most hearts, I think. Think flappers and Charlestonning the night away, and cars with runner boards and little biplanes and toffs with monocles and cocktails and feather boas and Satchmo and Fats and the joint jumpin' and wind-up gramophones with huge trumpets and Isadora Duncan with her scarf in the car wheel – (Scratch the last one.) Jazz bands are the thing for the perfect garden party.

Folk music

As I said earlier, I am a sucker for Scots ballads. In fact, I'm a sucker for all kinds of folk music from all over the world. I was moved to tears in a way I didn't quite understand when I saw the Haka performed by a group of Maoris in New Zealand. This said, I also cry at the sight of Morris dancers, something a VIK cannot relate to at all. Being a rugby devotee he finds it embarrassing that our great nation can only come up with a bunch of idiots with bells and ribbons and flowery hats and pig's bladders, while New Zealand gets the fearsomely intimidating and war-like Haka. I think he's forgetting the bits of stick the Morris men knock together. Those are pretty scary. They are certainly more workmanlike than the prissy Scottish dancing swords (see above, anti-Scots remarks).

CHAPTER 27
Collecting

Some people are snails who travel light through this world, carrying all their worldly goods on their back. Others are squirrels who gather and hoard things. If you are not sure which category you fall into, try this simple test. Go to your loft/cellar/cupboard under the stairs. If you can see the floor, you are a snail. This chapter is not for you, unless you want to read it out of a sort of morbid curiosity, to see how these strange people live who are incapable of chucking anything out. I read once of someone clearing out her dead mother's house and finding a paper bag labelled "Pieces of string too short to be of any use". She must have an *Über*-Squirrel, that woman.

NB. A true collector is not interested in the value of the things they collect. Their collection is *not* an investment against a rainy day.

What to collect

This really doesn't matter at all. The main thing is that you collect, and collect obsessively. My old room-mate from university days collects sugar packets, for instance. "Why?" is not a relevant question here. Over the years I have collected many things. When I was in my early teens I used to collect the "YES PLEASE!" stickers that catalogue companies used to send out. As in "YES PLEASE! Rush me my new thermal underwear catalogue!" I used to stick them in the back of my Bible. As a small child I was always buying old battered biscuit tins. Grown-ups would roll their eyes and say they didn't know why I wanted to waste my money on rubbish like that. I got the last laugh of course, because old battered biscuit tins are now highly collectable. These days I collect coloured glass from charity shops and church bazaars because I like to see the light shining through it. My sons collect empty crisp packets. Or so I surmise from the state of their bedrooms. A VIK collects amusing beer bottles called things like "Wicked Old Bishop's Peculiar Speckled Fart". And portraits of John Calvin.

One of the huge advantages of starting a collection is that people are never at a loss over what to buy you for Christmas. In fact, long after you feel that your collection of pottery hippopotamuses is complete, friends and family will continue adding to it, until you find yourself rather hoping to be burgled by a hippophile, or wishing you lived on a fault line so that the hippos could plunge lemming-like from the shelf during the next earthquake and you could start all over again with vintage cars.

Reasons to collect things

- because they look nice
- because less is never more
- because why not?
- in case they come in handy
- because you can't bring yourself to bin them

Accidental collecting

The last two reasons in the above list are dishonourable. Deliberate collecting, no matter how strange the thing collected, is a noble thing. Accidental collecting is mere accumulation and comes about through sloth or cowardice and should be resisted with true Christian vigour. I am talking about collections of supermarket receipts and pen lids on the one hand; and ugly vases and bath salts on the other – i.e. detritus and unwanted gifts.

Things you should not collect

- old hi-fis
- clapped-out shoes
- clothes you've grown out of
- chipped mugs
- little tubs of mouldy leftover food
- parking tickets
- stomach ulcers

Unwanted gifts and how to deal with them

There are few more delicate matters in our complex social world than gift giving. It is not only more blessed to give than to receive – it is also simpler. If you are the giver, you don't have to compose your features into an expression of pleasure when you unwrap your inspirational statuette of Jesus playing baseball.[1] The main thing to do is focus on the love and thoughtfulness which went behind the gift. I have a dear friend who has mastered the art of saying "Oh!" in tones of such delighted surprise and discovery that no words are really needed. The phrase "You shouldn't have!" is also handy (as in You *really* shouldn't have).

I know there are some people who believe that honesty is the best policy. This was my Grandma's stance. She always greeted presents with the stock phrase: "Wherever shall I put it?"[2] Honesty is the best policy, indeed! This is a scurrilous motto to adopt. Honesty should be embraced for its own sake, not for any political reason. Being kind is more important than any spurious sense of personal integrity, here. Of course, there is always the danger that your enthusiastic gratitude may result in a whole collection of inspirational statues of the Sporting Jesus; but that is a risk you will have to take.

Kindness does not extend to having to keep every gift you ever receive, however. Don't be intimidated into hanging pictures you hate on the slim off-chance that Aunty Dora will call round and check up on you.

Occasionally people will follow up unwanted gifts with even more unwelcome enquiries. "Do you ever use that oven glove embroidered with Psalm 23 I gave you?" your acquaintance will ask bluntly. At this point temporary global amnesia will descend and the question "*What* oven glove embroidered with Psalm 23?" will echo round the dusty wastes of your brain. Don't fritter away valuable time trying to remember, just lay a hand warmly on their arm, look them in the eye and say "Oh, that was *so* kind of you! Do you know, I think

---

1. I did not just make that up, by the way. Check it out on the internet.

2. You can only hear this response so many times without being tempted to buy the person a packet of suppositories.

of you every time I use it!" This is not lying. This is what we call in the vicarage "Good Stewardship of facts".

Remember: Life is too short for moulded glass relish trays.

The theology of collecting

What does the Bible have to say on this subject? Jesus told a parable warning against the dangers of greedily hoarding this world's treasures into bigger barns. I think we can look to Noah's ark as a good positive example of collecting – male and female of every species, because they were worth saving. I think collecting is all about relishing both variety and order, and these are both very god-like traits. If we take my glass fetish, for example, we can see both the range of different colours (red, pale blue, cobalt, turquoise, green, amber), and styles (cups, saucers, vases, candlesticks) and the single uniting fact that they are all made of glass – and cost next to nothing and in any case, the money went to a good cause. Not that I'm feeling defensive, or anything.

CHAPTER 28
Perfect sense

When I was young my friends and I didn't need expensive computer games to keep us occupied. We amused ourselves by jumping on and off the conveyor belts in the local quarry or chucking bits of mortar into our neighbour's immaculate garden.[1] Occasionally we played on the railway lines. Even if the weather kept us cooped up indoors, we didn't need electronic gadgets to keep boredom at bay. We played all sorts of imaginative games. One of them involved posing ourselves the question, Would you rather be deaf or blind?

Most of us have wondered from time to time which of our five (if we are blessed with a full complement) senses we could most readily dispense with. Most people nominate their sense of smell. This is a pretty pointless exercise, really, and you'd be better off chucking mortar, except for the reminder it gives us of how much pleasure and information our different senses give us.

Perfect sight

Now this is an area I am not competent to speak about. I have only met one person more short-sighted than I am, and I must say I felt obscurely robbed. I have no idea what it's like to wake up and be able to see clearly. I suppose I must have been able to as a small child, but for as long as I can remember, the world has been blurred. Like most short-sighted children I assumed this was normal. It wasn't until I walked out of the opticians wearing my very first pair of blue plastic National Health Service glasses that I realised grass was made up of individual blades and roof edges were sharp and crisp against the sky.

---

1. This game was instigated by my older sister with the words "Anyone who doesn't get it into Mr Routledge's garden is a duck!" On one occasion Mr Routledge caught us, and very sportingly joined in, throwing it all back into our garden while we cowered in the shed.

It was almost worth being short-sighted just to have that experience of blundering out into a new and wondrous universe. Surely heaven will be like that. We sense it there sometimes, catch it out of the corner of our eye, feel that if we could only peel the surface back we'd find it there waiting to greet us.

Being short-sighted makes you acutely aware of the shortcomings of those with 20/20 vision. Not long after you sally forth in your first spectacles you are forced to confront the intellectual laziness and sorry lack of imagination of those around you. People have been wearing glasses for centuries, but nobody has yet come up with an alternative to "Four eyes!" as an insult. That's a bit like calling Pinocchio "Big nose!" isn't it?

Perfect vision isn't everything. It ain't what you see, it's the way that you see it. To get the best out of your eyes, you need to stop and stare. You need to look up at the roof tops, you need to watch the sky. You need to walk, not drive. You need not to be in a hurry all the time. Sit with a cappuccino and watch the world go by. Hoard up colours in your memory. The green of the first beech leaves unfolding, the white of a gull against the sky, the strange electric blue of delphiniums in the dusk.

When I was at Infant School we used to sing a hymn that went "Be careful little eyes what you see/Oh be careful little eyes what you see/There's a Father up above looking down with tender love/So be careful little eyes what you see." I'm sure I wasn't the only child who took that to mean I wasn't to look at naughty stuff or read my sister's diary. The same went for the little ears and hands and feet in the rest of the hymn. I bet that most Evangelicals would interpret "good stewardship of the eyes" in terms of prohibition, not permission. No porn, rather than relishing the world of light and colour. We're a sad bunch, aren't we?

Perfect hearing

When children are tiny they are given hearing tests by health visitors who jingle keys and whisper the child's name to see if it looks round. I think they could usefully include the sound of rustling cellophane in the test. A child must truly have ear trouble if it cannot hear its mother trying stealthily to open a bar of chocolate half a mile away behind closed doors. My hearing is not what it once was. I used to be able to hear bats calling. I can't any more. I put this down to too much vacuuming. It ruins your ears. I also suffer from temporary deafness when I am reading, as my sons will testify.

People have always looked to their sense of hearing to enhance their lives (see above, Chapter 26 on music). These days there is a fashion for helping ease urban stress with the sound of gently running water. Many people have little indoor fountains constantly playing. This is the sound of a little mountain stream playing over pebbles, people tell themselves. Would they love it as much if you told them it was the sound of the sewage out-fall into the Mersey? Possibly not, although the sound itself would be the same. Association is all.

Happy sounds are those we associate with happy times. The distant sound of church bells, the song of the sky lark, the roar of the Toon Army when Newcastle thrash Man U. But in order for those sounds to cheer your soul, you have to have registered them at some earlier stage. Take time to listen to the dawn chorus, to fine music, to the wind in the trees and the waves on the shore.

Sounds to edit out

- drunken voices in the night
- other people's radios
- mosquitoes
- knee joints cracking
- other people's children

Perfect taste

Good coffee, good wine, fresh fish, meat from your butcher and not the supermarket, home-baking, ripe fruit and cheese, Belgian chocolates. Make up your own list. But here's my motto: eat less better. Fortunately, good doesn't automatically mean expensive. Don't bother with rubbish. Garbage in, waistline out. We live in a finite world, so the very best mouthful is always going to be the first. Anticipate it, postpone it, savour it, look back on it. I can still remember my first encounter with a New Zealand *sauvignon blanc*. I was at a party in England before we ever set foot in the southern hemisphere. I took a mouthful, and was rocked back in my seat. "Now

*"Well it's not soothing the dog! That's the third 'walkies'
he's taken by the lampstand this morning."*

that," I said, turning to the man next to me, "is a fantastic wine."
"Good," he replied. "I was the one who advised our hosts to buy it."
Think how much worse that little exchange could have gone.

Perfect touch

These days I'm a real country mouse. I sometimes get up to London
and when I do, I like to visit Liberty's so that I can gasp in that
Aladdin's cave of consumer bliss – and reel back in shock at the prices.
My favourite thing is touching the merchandise, digging my fingers
rapturously into the plush of the carpet bags, stroking the devoré
velvet scarves and burying my face in the cashmere sweaters and
getting escorted off the premises and told not to come back. Do it, I
urge you! Baby's foreheads, cat's fur, polished wood, group hugs –
enjoy!

Perfect smell

Freshly ground coffee, tomato leaves, sweet peas, wood smoke,
honeysuckle on a summer night. You don't need me here. Scent is a
deeply person thing with a very private set of significances. My sons
like the smell of petrol, for instance. I like the smell of creosote fences
in the sunshine. Most of us have been caught at some point in our
lives with our heads hanging a little too greedily over a bowl of
something delicious, inhaling in bliss. I like to think that this is what
the Bible is talking about when it likens prayer to the rising fumes of
incense. Do the divine nostrils metaphorically flare with a satisfied
"Aaah!"?

CHAPTER 29
How to write

*I*n this chapter I will spill the beans on various closely guarded secrets of the writing profession, enabling you to write bestsellers and make your fortune, the way I have done so successfully myself.

The above promise was an example of the fiction writer's skill. Contrary to popular belief, most novelists earn a pittance. I could make more cleaning offices, to be honest; but I wouldn't have as much fun. Writing comes in various forms. We will tackle a few of them in turn.

How to write the perfect sermon

The more time you devote to your sermon preparation, the better the sermon will be. Unfortunately, sermon preparation often gets squeezed out in a pastor's busy week. The **Important** always gives way to the **Urgent**, however trivial and frustrating the urgent may be. How often does the minister find him or herself dealing with the Broken Tea Urn Crisis, rather than sitting in their study reading and pondering? This is why you must must *must* enter "Sermon preparation" into your diary and consider it as unalterable an appointment as "Funeral, crem 10am".

Perfect sermon checklist

Your sermon should be

- thought-provoking
- well-prepared
- intelligent
- inspiring
- funny

Failing that it should be

• short

If your sermon is basically a piece of Bible exposition, make sure you are actually preaching from the text in front of you, not imposing your own personal gospel formula on it. A sermon on Cain and Abel does not have to have a "Man's Sin, God's Solution" conclusion clapped onto the end to make it valid.

This is fun! A rare opportunity to preach at the preachers.

The main thing to remember when you are writing your sermon is that the Holy Spirit will be the one who speaks to people's hearts, not you. Occasionally the Holy Spirit seems to be using a different script. A VIK often has the experience of being thanked for that helpful thing he said, when to the best of his recollection he has said no such thing. If this happens to you, incline your head in a gracious pastoral way and take the credit.

I have occasionally accepted preaching engagements, but just between you and me, I hate preaching. I can't restrain the impulse to try to be funny. This is OK, except when nobody laughs. Standing up there in the pulpit looking out over pews full of stony faces is a very lonely and desolate experience.[1] If this is how you feel about preaching, you might like to ask yourself if you are working in the right medium.

After-dinner speaking

This is much easier than preaching because your audience will be drunk and will laugh at anything. I generally find that if I say "vicar" and then, in my hilarious way, follow up with the word "knicker", I will get a standing ovation. Unless they are too sozzled to stand, in which case they bang the table with their fists before slumping face down into their Stilton. There are not many church congregations this convivial – although St Paul's, Walsall comes close. A curate I know began a Christmas sermon with the assertion, "A Christingle is not a pantomime." To which we all – without being primed beforehand –

---

1. It is what a poet I know describes as the "tumbleweed blowing across the desert" moment which he gets when he has just finished reading a poem out loud to an audience.

chorused "OH YES IT IS!" This is unusual within Anglicanism, where the sermon is usually seen as an opportunity to think about gardening.

After-dinner speaking has one main requirement. You have to be amusing. There are two basic approaches to being funny. One is to string together a series of set comic pieces or jokes which you have collected over the years. This has two risks attached. Firstly, the audience may have already heard your gags from someone else. Secondly, if you flag up the joke too obviously (Huge punchline coming, listen, you'll like this one, it'll kill you, here it comes! Ready?), there's more chance of it falling flat. The other approach, the one I favour myself, is the dead-pan anecdotal "a funny thing happened to me in the vestry" style.

The only downside of after-dinner speaking is getting through the interminable meal that precedes it, too sick with nerves to eat and too scared of losing control of your anecdotes to drink.

Remember the golden rule: Don't Drink and Speak.

How to write the perfect novel

The most important thing to remember when writing a novel is to keep the reader's interest. There's not much point being brilliant, experimental and toweringly intellectual if people fall asleep reading you. Personally, I like a novel with a cracking good story, interesting characterisation and good dialogue. Work hard on these three things. They are the foundation stones of good fiction.

If you are writing a perfect *Christian* novel, there are three more things to remember:

- no swearing
- no explicit sex
- convert everyone by the end

If you are serious about wanting to write for publication, get on a writing course. This will give you a great boost. Keep a journal. Read, read, read. Apart from these bits of advice, there is unfortunately only one secret to being a writer – getting on and writing the stuff.

How to write poetry

Let me be candid here. I have no idea, otherwise I'd write some. I can churn out tum-te-tum rhyming stuff and spoofs and pastiches, but the art of true poetry is beyond me. It is a gift. Some people have the gift of inspiring poetry in others. A VIK has been given many devotional poems during his ministry, although I can't help wondering if these are tailing off as the years go by.

Letter writing

Thank you letters

These are growing less and less common. My advice is that you don't take offence if people fail to send you one. It doesn't mean they aren't grateful. It just means they are less polite than you are.

Fan letters to writers

People often worry that when they write appreciative letters to authors their own writing style will seem inadequate. Don't worry. No writer is troubled by praise. Just to help you, here's a sample of what would be considered acceptable:

"Dear X, I just want to say how much I love your work. I am enclosing £1000/crate of champagne/holiday in Tuscan villa as a token of my regard. Sincerely."

Hate mail to writers

Green Biro is traditional here. Make sure you gouge deeply into the paper to express your anger. Use block capitals and inverted commas round the author's name on the envelope to imply "the so-called 'CATHERINE FOX' (sneer, sneer)".

CHAPTER 30
How to be organised

Being organised is a simple matter of following two guidelines:

- make lists
- never procrastinate

If you are sitting looking at these rules and thinking, "Yes, I must get round to making a list sometime," then you can be sure that you are not an organised person. And hands up if you are reading this book when you should be doing something else. Have you been thinking "I'll just read one more chapter and then I'll tidy up/emerge from the loo/turn the light off and get some sleep"? If so, why, thank you! There's nothing more flattering to a writer's ego than the knowledge that her book is a displacement activity. And frankly, who *cares* about being organised?

Sadly, there are times when we must all get a grip on our lives and sort ourselves out. Tax returns have to be filled in. PE kits must be found. It's a question of getting to the point when it is more bearable to tackle these irksome tasks than to endure the background anxiety that goes with leaving them undone.

I have several warning signs that tell me to procrastinate no longer.

Mail Dread Syndrome. This is when you are convinced that the post will include an official looking window envelope and a scary letter containing phrases like IT HAS COME TO OUR ATTENTION and KINDLY RECTIFY THIS SITUATION IMMEDIATELY. After I have dealt with all my deferred tasks I'm much more likely to approach the doormat jauntily to see if there are unexpected cheques or exciting parcels instead.

Nightmares. Another warning sign is the "starved pet in the attic" dream I get when I'm stressed. I was interested to discover one of my sisters has the same dream. She shakes her husband awake in panic, begging him to reassure her they don't own a parrot.

Stress-related illness. But perhaps my favourite shot across the bows from my subconscious is the migraine. I tend to get these when there are several medium-sized things troubling me, none of them urgent or awful enough in their own right to merit immediate action. Over the years I've been learning to recognise the signs and pre-empt the attack by dealing with my correspondence and filling in forms, etc. before too much mounts up. Failing that, I console myself with the thought that migraines are probably nature's way of stopping you getting stomach ulcers.

Organising your home

The big tidy and clear-out generally happens in the vicarage every five years or so when we move house, but you can tackle the job any time. It can be a very good displacement activity for, say, root canal fillings. And like visits to the dentist, you will feel very much better when it's all over.

When trying to sort through your life's clutter, don't ask "Can I imagine circumstances under which I might possibly need this item?" This is no guide at all, because most of us are secretly worried that the minute we chuck away the forty empty jam jars we've kept under the sink for eight years, there will promptly be a world glass shortage and we will simultaneously be seized by the urge to make damson jam. Instead, ask yourself if you have used the item in the last year. If not, chuck it.

I never do this. But this is OK. I am merely telling you how to be perfect, not claiming to have achieved perfection.

Plastic baskets

Here in the vicarage we are great believers in having lots and lots of little plastic baskets for putting things in. About once every three years a VIK tidies the tool cupboard. This involves a happy day of sorting screws and curtain hooks and scraps of used sandpaper into their proper categories and then putting them in their own little plastic basket. The baskets are then arranged neatly on the shelves. I am invited to come and admire the tool cupboard. Sadly, this newly imposed order only lasts about a month. This is because on any given occasion it is quicker simply to chuck the screwdriver or paintbrush into the nearest little basket than track down the correct one and file it away properly.

Things for putting things in

There are a great many companies devoted to selling us things for putting things in. You can buy cloth tubes for putting used carrier bags in (good idea), plastic dividers for your sock draw to keep your socks each in their own little separate nest (odd idea) and plastic containers for you to pour your cereal into, out of their perfectly serviceable cardboard boxes (stupid idea). The companies who produce this merchandise know that we are all vaguely seeking salvation through organisation. At some level we believe that if we can impose order on the chaos that is our sock drawer, somehow harmony will be restored to our dislocated lives. But the truth is, if we have enough time to post our socks into their individual cubby holes, we have enough time to rootle about and find a matching pair.

Organising your cutlery drawer

There is a non-negotiable cosmic law that states you must organise your cutlery draw from left to right in the following order – knives, forks, spoons. Even on Mars this obtains. If you have been transgressing this rule for years and your life has been unhappy, then look no further for an explanation. Spoons, knives, forks is asking for trouble. It is as illogical as spring, summer, winter, autumn. You are violating the language of the eternal spheres, and if I ever visit your house, I will personally rearrange your cutlery for you to avert financial ruin and flooding.

Organising your knick-knacks

My mother has an inviolable rule that ornaments on mantelpieces and shelves must not be arranged symmetrically. I sometimes arrange them that way to annoy her. Her other rule is that jugs must point towards the centre of the shelf, with their handles turned outwards. If you have tiny children the formula to remember is that they can reach x+20cm, where *x* is the distance you *think* they can reach.

The mug rack dilemma

I have a mug rack which is capable of holding about one third of the mugs we own. I like to keep the nicest mugs on the rack where people can see them, and shove the chipped horrible ones in the cupboard. So far so good. But people come along and use the nice mugs, leaving a gap on the rack. This is problematical. I don't want to fill the gap with a horrible mug, but if I leave a gap, then I have a non-functioning hook. The alternative is to have non-functioning mugs which are there for decoration only. Perhaps the solution is to drop all the ghastly mugs accidentally, and replace them with nice ones, so that it doesn't matter which ones are on display.

The trouble is, I need nasty mugs for church meetings. I also need them for when people come to the door for sandwiches and a cup of tea. My first thought is that I'm not using my nice mugs in case they get pinched. My second that this is unworthy and that I should give them china. And I shouldn't give them stale cheese, I should give them that smoked salmon I was saving for myself. WWJD? But they probably don't like smoked salmon. So I give them cheese, but use butter instead of cheap marge, and put a packet of crisps and a chocolate biscuit in as a sort of compromise, knowing that one of my sons won't have a chocolate biscuit in his packed lunch tomorrow, but WWJD, darling? He'd give his biscuit away! I also add an apple, because of the vitamins and anti-oxidants it contains. And at the last moment I give way to a petty impulse and serve the tea in a horrible cup after all, in the hopes that it gets pinched. Bad person.

Ten organisational strategies I never actually carry out

1.   Putting receipts in a safe place so I can find them when I want to take something back to the shop.

2. Putting work expense receipts in a safe place ready for my tax return.
3. Dealing with correspondence on a regular basis.
4. Reading and absorbing the contents of letters from school so as not to be caught out by staff training days.
5. Throwing away lids of plastic containers when I've lost the container.
6. Throwing away old bibles.
7. Culling the soft toys.
8. Disposing of beans and pulses when they are more than 20 years old.
9. Putting photos in albums.
10. Making a note of birthdays so I can send presents to godchildren in the right quarter of the year.

Dear Reader—
Sorry about lack of cartoon but felt really guilty about strategies 1 to 4 and 10 on the list. If not back in 10 minutes please feel free to indulge in some interactive illustration with the tools provided.

0.1 Permanent Ink

HB

eraser

"11. Deal with stains promptly or alternatively always replace pen cap after use."

The perfect end

This is something that people with a Compline[1] habit pray for regularly. "The Lord Almighty grant us a quiet night and perfect end." Occasionally, in my shallow way, I find myself sort of diverting the intent of this prayer and mentally inserting the word "rear" before the word "end". Shame on me. But we are not here to ask "Does my bum look big in this pew?"

What does "a perfect end" constitute? Clearly it refers to the end of our life. It is a prayer for the blessing mentioned in the old Prayer Book Litany[2], that we might be delivered from "sudden death", or dying unprepared. I will mention our grand old Puritan forebears one last time, and their attempts to live each day as though it were their last. In our guilt-racked Evangelical way we tend to think of this in terms of not living in sin, or with a clutter of moral debt weighing us down. Short accounts with God! Clean spiritual underwear in case we get mown down by death and trolleyed in to the great A & E in the sky!

Let's just lay aside the *proper* answers for a moment and ask, What would I most regret if I were to die tonight? For me it would be not living to see my beloved boys grow up to be men. Where our imagined regrets lie is where we should be living now. I cannot fend off death. There are no brilliant novels I could write or delicious cakes I could bake, there are no judo throws, no witty asides, personal charm, no deals I could broker, *nothing* I can do that would stave off mortality. But I *can* live my life in such a way that if I were to die suddenly and too soon, then my sons would know for sure that this, *this* is what I was like – unmistakably, uniquely, to the full. Not perfect, but still a star.

---

1. The office of Night Prayer.

2. A type of prayer consisting of a list of invocations followed by a set response. **Invocation:** "Lord, we really just want to thank you, Father." **Response:** "Mmm. Yes, Lord. Mmm." This would be an example of a litany.

Don't defer being that quintessence of you until some distant future where you are thin, or rich, or happy, or truly spiritual, or in heaven. What you have is like the precious ointment in the Gospel. Pour it out. Let the perfume fill the whole house. If it's for our Lord, it is never wasted.

"Ahh, isn't that nice! They help you pack your bags if you've got a lot of stuff."